This Week in Estes Park: The Story of Our Town

By Mel Busch

Edited by Andrew and Melinda Busch

THIS WEEK IN ESTES PARK: THE STORY OF OUR TOWN by Mel Busch (Edited by Andrew and Melinda Busch)

This book or parts thereof may not be reproduced in any form, stored in a retrieval system, or transmitted in any form by any means—electronic, mechanical, photocopy, recording, or otherwise—without prior written permission of the publisher, except as provided by United States copyright law.

Copyright © 2018 by Andrew E. Busch.
All rights reserved.

International Standard Book Number 978-0-692-18183-6

Cover image of the Longs Peak Inn courtesy of Estes Park Museum, 1985.088.001.

Articles reprinted by permission of *Estes Park Trail-Gazette*.

Note from the editors: We would like to thank Derek Fontini and Jessica Michak of the Estes Park Museum for their assistance and encouragement, Marionette Moore for her cover design, and the staff at IngramSpark for their production assistance.

This Week in Estes Park:
The Story of Our Town

Preface vii
JANUARY 1
   Popular Recipes of Yesteryear 2
   Triumph and Tragedy in the Snow 7
   Radioitis Epidemic Hits Estes 11
   Olympic Jumper Hometown Hero 15
   Enos Mills: Father of Rocky Mountain National Park 19
FEBRUARY 23
   Canyon Highway History 24
   Estes Park's Irish Land Baron 28
   Estes Park: Ski Mecca? 32
   Estes Park's Firstborn Arrived in 6th Year of Local Settlement 35
MARCH 39
   Estes Park Fire Gear Didn't Come Easy 40
   Estes Park's Notable Women 44
   Founder of Moraine Lodge Died in 1928 48
   Deaths Led to Shelter Cabin 52
   Happy Birthday, Abner 56
APRIL 59
   Enos Mills Promoted Conservation 60
   Illustrating Early Estes 66
   Newspaper Life Since 1908 70
   How the Village Became a Town 75
MAY 79
   Presbyterians and the 'Devil' 80

Sheriff, Realtor, Benefactor..83
Music: A Timeless Attraction 87
The Lake Slept in Silence 91
JUNE..95
An Earlier 'Confluence Park'...96
Shootout in Muggins Gulch Spawns Mountain Jim Legend 100
Jim Dies Repeatedly; Story Keeps Changing................105
Stanley's Genius Evident Early......................................110
An Elegant Hotel Opens Its Doors 117
Long's Sighting of Highest Peak....................................122
JULY 127
Estes Family's 'Pioneer Day' Reunion 128
Retracing Our Indian Heritage......................................133
Western 'Stampede' Launched Rodeo Tradition 138
Toll Road Offered Estes Park – Lyons Link..................144
AUGUST..149
Famous Friendship Founded in EP 150
Misguided Souls in 'Elkanah Valley' Received Inspiration (and Damnation) from Rev. Lamb................................156
'New' Trail Improved Access to Longs Peak via Chasm Lake 161
Climbing Longs Peak in 1868 165
SEPTEMBER 169
Parting Vision of Rocky Mountain Jim........................170
Improvement Association Left Fishy Legacy................174
Estes Park Given Its Name 180
Seasonal Rites Endure 182
Estes Park's First Press Agent 186

OCTOBER 189
  Birth of a Valiant Lady 190
  Isabella Bird's Worldly Travels....................................... 194
  Gentlemen Are Born, Not Made 198
  How the Museum Evolved 202
  Ferguson, Hubbell First EP Newlyweds 205
NOVEMBER 209
  Community Church of Rockies Moves—But Not Too
  Quickly 210
  Stanley Sale Ended Grand Era 214
  Local Political Trends 218
  Misunderstood Resident Pioneered Propaganda Analysis
  221
  Thanksgiving Homestead 225
  Buel Porter's Christmas Legacy 229
DECEMBER 233
  Twists of History Led to Library.................................... 234
  The Secret to Shaping Young Minds 237
  Early Electrical Woes.. 241
  A Guide for All Seasons 243
  Abner Sprague's 1930 New Year's Resolution 246
BIBLIOGRAPHY 249
INDEX 251

Preface

My father, Melvin Busch, started as the Curator at the Estes Park Area Historical Museum in June 1978. The Museum was small, his job was part-time, and he was making a big career change. Since leaving the Air Force in 1957, he had been employed in the technical field, most recently working for a decade and a half calibrating instruments on airplanes for weather experiments conducted by the National Center for Atmospheric Research. Although he was skilled in this work, he did not find it fulfilling. His real love was western history.

Contemplating a life change, in his forties Dad got a degree in history from Loretto Heights University in Denver and then took some graduate courses in museum studies at the University of Colorado. When he heard about the opportunity in Estes Park, he jumped at it. He threw himself into the job, and within a few years the Museum had a full-time Director. He worked at the Museum from 1978 to 1991, when early-onset Alzheimer's forced his premature retirement. The first five years, our family continued living in Boulder, so Dad lived at the Museum four days a week, sleeping on a cot in the office area. Mom and Dad moved to Estes Park in 1984.

One of the first things Dad did at the Museum was to launch a fundraising drive to buy the Stanley Steamer that is still on proud display. Under Dad's leadership, the Museum also added several rooms to its main building, professionalized both its exhibits and its storage of materials, became a great educational resource for the community, and acquired and restored the Cobb-MacDonald Cabin and the first Rocky Mountain National Park headquarters building.

He loved teaching about the history of Estes Park. Few things delighted him more than talking with school groups, but he also used the written word to sketch the colorful story of the Estes Valley and environs. For several years in the early 1980s, Dad penned a regular column for the *Estes Park Trail-Gazette*—sometimes monthly, sometimes weekly—on timely topics in Estes Park history. On occasion, he would also write longer features for the *Trail-Gazette's* vacation edition. These windows into the past were drawn from exploration into long-past issues of the newspaper, memoirs of participants, and public records. They were sometimes poignant, sometimes funny, and always informative.

A number of these articles have finally been brought together in this collection, an effort that my wife, Melinda, and I began more than 20 years ago. We have lightly edited the articles and have drawn from both the published versions and the original manuscripts. Together, they provide an entertaining picture of Estes Park through the years. I would also like to think that this collection is a small tribute to the role Mel Busch played in the development of the Museum and the preservation of Estes Park's history.

Written as newspaper columns, these articles are highly accessible but lack footnotes. Generally, Dad did take pains to identify his sources in the columns, and

Preface ix

we have compiled these into a bibliography at the back of the book. We have also supplied an index for the reader's convenience.

These articles represent Dad's best effort to convey history as it was recorded in newspaper accounts and personal memoirs, but those accounts themselves may not be perfect. Sometimes they even conflict, as in the competing memories of "Mountain Jim" Nugent's death, which Dad recounted and left to the reader to assess. History is always an ongoing process of discovery as more information and new interpretations emerge.

Dad passed away from complications of Alzheimer's on November 11, 1999, at the Veterans Administration home in Florence, Colorado. In May 2015, I had the honor, with my family, of accepting on Dad's behalf the Pioneer Award given by the Estes Park Museum Friends & Foundation in recognition of his service.

I hope you enjoy reading these articles as much as he enjoyed writing them!

    Andrew E. Busch
    September 2018

JANUARY

Popular Recipes of Yesteryear

While scanning publications and records for this week in our history I ran across the following article in the January 3, 1936 *Trail.*

"A new cook book, prepared by the Ladies Aid and printed by the *Trail,* containing tested recipes for high altitude cooking goes on sale this week-end.

"The 104-page book contains about 250 of the favorite recipes of about 50 housewives of the region. Every type of dish is described.

"The cook book will probably be placed on sale in the stores and is expected to prove especially helpful to summer visitors who find their low-altitude recipes failing.

"Five hundred copies of the book have been printed.

"Mrs. Walter Fulton, editor, and Mrs. Guy Albright, assistant editor, directed the publication. It will sell for 50 cents per copy."

We do not have the space to repeat all the recipes, and there is no way that I will claim to have picked the best of the many, many mouth-watering offerings, but I pulled out one from each of several sections of the book for you to either try or dream about.

Soups: My Mother's Vegetable Soup—Mrs. L.S. Hall
A good-sized knuckle bone
½ cup of pearl barley
Put on stove in large kettle and cover well with cold

January 3

water

Let come to boil and boil for 1 ½ hours Then add:

1 ½ medium sized cabbage—shredded

5 or 6 good sized carrots diced very small

Let boil ½ hour with salt and pepper to bring out flavor. Add more water if desired. This makes 4 or 5 quarts of soup. Is better when re-heated. Two or three pounds of boiling meat may be cooked at the same time.

One-dish meals: Sausage Dinner Treat—Nellie Mancell

Boil three large sweet potatoes until tender, then peel and cut in halves lengthwise. In a shallow baking dish place the potatoes. Cover with par-boiled sausage (linked), two or three to each potato, and sliced apples. Sprinkle with one-fourth cup of brown sugar and add the pork drippings which have been boiled up with one-quarter cup of water. Cover the dish and bake in a moderate oven for 30 minutes. Serves four or five.

Meats: Caramel Meat Loaf—Mrs. Walter Fulton 1 lb. ground beef

1 lb. ground pork

½ lb. ground ham

Soak 2 slices white bread in 1 cup milk and add 1 ½ tsp. mustard, and 1 or 2 eggs. Mix well together and put in loaves and cover with brown sugar and whole cloves. Bake in slow oven two hours.

Vegetables: Mystery chef's way of cooking cabbage, cauliflower without odor, improving the appearance, flavor, and digestibility of the vegetable—Mrs. S.M. Hurd

Start in boiling water and leave the kettle uncovered; do not put a lid on.

Cut up vegetables not very fine.

Put two pots of water on the stove and bring them to a boil. Now into one pot put a teaspoon of baking soda, then add vegetable. Let it boil in this only 3 minutes, no longer. Strain the water off, then place the vegetable in the other pot of water. Add salt and allow to boil until tender.

Cheese and Egg Dishes: Cheese Puff—Mrs. A.E. Sprague. 4 slices of bread

1 C. American cheese, grated 2 raw eggs

1 ¼ C. milk ½ tsp. salt

Put a slice of bread in a buttered baking dish, cover with cheese, another slice, etc., until all are used. Beat eggs, add milk and salt and pour over bread and cheese and bake about 30 minutes.

Bread: Nut Bread (2loaves)—Mrs. F.P. Clatworthy 1 ½ cups sugar

2 eggs

1 ½ cups milk 1 cup nut meats

4 tsp. baking powder 4 cups flour

Salt

No shortening

Let set 30 minutes and bake til done.

Cake: Chocolate yeast cake—Mrs. Roy Baldwin 2 C. sugar—creamed

1 C. shortening

3 eggs

1 C. milk 3 C. flour

1 cake Fleischmann's yeast dissolved in ¼ cup warm water

3 squares melted chocolate 1 C. chopped nuts

Mix well and let rise over night. Then add 1 tsp. soda dissolved in 3 T. boiling water and 1 tsp. vanilla. Bake

January

in moderate oven 45 minutes.

Cookies: Filled Oatmeal Cookies—Mrs. E.C. Loy
Cook together:
1 pound of dates 1 cup of water 2/3 cup of sugar
Boil and stir until it forms a smooth paste.

Cream 1 cup of shortening, 1 cup of sugar, add 1 egg well beaten, 1 ½ cup of sour milk, 2 cups of ground oatmeal, 2 cups of white flour, 1 ½ teaspoon of salt, 1 teaspoon of soda, 2 teaspoons of baking powder. Roll dough thin, cut cookies, place a spoonful of paste between two cookies, press down edges and cook in moderate oven.

Pies: Angel Food Pie—Mrs. Carmen Johnson
1 ½ cups sugar
2 cups water
3 heaping tbsp. com starch
Cook til clear, not thick. 3 egg whites beaten stiff.

Pour the above slowly into the whites. Beat five minutes with egg beater. Add vanilla. Fill baked pie shells, cover with coconut. Over this spread whipped cream and let stand 6 hours.

Candy: Fruit Balls—Mrs. N.E. Ogier
Equal parts of raisins, figs, apricots, prunes, dates. Grind all. Mix with lemon juice and roll in powdered sugar. Very good for children.

Preserves and Pickles: Preserved Strawberries—Hazel E. Cheney

Measure 2 quarts strawberries, scald 2 minutes in hot water. Pour off water. Add 4 cups sugar and boil 2 minutes after it bubbles. Remove from fire. When bubbling stops add 2 cups sugar and boil 5 minutes. Count time as specified. Pour in shallow pan 1 ½ to 2 inches deep. Let stand all night and can cold the next morning.

> As the ladies said in the preface of their book:
> "Problems of state confront the great
> And love is bitter sweet,
> But the question that perplexes us,
> And worries us and vexes us,
> Far more than love or politics,
> Is simply—What to eat?"

[January 4, 1984]

Triumph and Tragedy in the Snow

On Saturday afternoon, January 10, 1925, an automobile carrying three people left Denver for the Estes Park area. The two passengers were Miss Elinor Eppich and Walter Kiener. Mr. Kiener, an experienced mountaineer from Switzerland, had been in the United States for three years. The driver and owner of the car was Miss Agnes Wolcott Vaille. She had climbed most of the difficult peaks in the state and many in the United States. The previous year she had scaled James Peak alone in the dead of winter. All three were Colorado Mountain Club members.

They made it as far as the Baldpate Inn, but the snow was too deep to drive further so they left the car and snowshoed on to Longs Peak Inn, and beyond to Timberline Cabin. It was then three o'clock Sunday morning.

Let's back-track a little to this week in our history three years earlier when Ranger Jack Moomaw made the first known winter ascent of Longs Peak. Since he had gone up the south side on January 9, 1922 no other winter trip to the top had been accomplished.

The first attempt on the east face of Longs was in September of 1922, when James W. Alexander, a math professor at Princeton University, accomplished that climb. A couple days later Jack Moomaw accompanied Professor Alexander up the east face taking pictures.

That side of Longs had been conquered only a few times (summer only) during the next two years when Agnes Vaille decided she wanted to combine those two feats and make a winter ascent up the east face of Longs Peak.

She and Walter Kiener left Timberline Cabin about 9 a.m. Sunday, reached Chasm Lake with no difficulty, and began the ascent. Miss Eppich went back to Longs Peak Inn to wait for them. By sundown they were only half way to the top, and by the time the summit was reached at 4 a.m. Monday, they and the peak were enveloped in a raging storm.

They decided to immediately descend the north side, nearest to Timberline Cabin and Longs Peak Inn. Miss Vaille slipped on the icy rocks and slid down for about 150 feet. She seemed to be more exhausted than hurt.

After assisting her to a sheltered spot in the upper end of Boulder Field, Kiener left at her insistence to go for aid. He left at 10:30 a.m. and reached Timberline Cabin at 1:30 p.m.

When the two had not returned Monday morning, Elinor Eppich, Herbert Sortland, caretaker of Longs Peak Inn, Hugh Brown, his son Oscar, and Jac Christen who were putting up ice at the Inn headed for Timberline.

When Kiener reached the cabin, Miss Eppich had gone back to the Inn to contact Park Superintendent Roger Toll, and the men were ready to begin their search. Oscar Brown was sent back to Longs Peak Inn with the latest news, and the rest left for the rescue.

An exhausted Sortland turned back near Granite Pass, and soon the older Brown headed 'for the cabin to keep a good fire going for the return of the others. He did not see Herbert Sortland on the way.

When Kiener and Christen reached Boulder Field they found Miss Vaille dead. It was after 4 p.m., Kiener's thermometer read 50 below zero, and a heavy sleet was covering them with a sheet of ice. It was impossible for the two to bring the body out at that time, and they returned to the cabin. Kiener's hands and feet were frozen by that time.

While waiting for the weather to clear enough to retrieve Agnes Vaille's remains, the search continued for Herbert Sortland.

Walter Finn, Superintendent Toll, Chief Ranger T.J. Allen, Ranger Jack Moomaw, experienced guides Jack Dillon and Warren Rutledge, and President Edmund Rogers and other members of the Colorado Mountain Club were all involved in the rescue attempt.

On Thursday, January 15, a party with skis and a toboggan left the Inn at 5 a.m. and returned after dark with Miss Vaille's body.

On February 25, Oscar Brown, now caretaker of Longs Peak Inn, accidentally discovered the body of Herbert Sortland about 300 yards southeast of the Inn.

The April 17, 1925, *Estes Park Trail* states that Walter Kiener "...was discharged from the hospital last week fully recovered from his experiences so far as will ever be possible.

"Mr. Keiner suffered the loss of all the fingers and most of the thumb of the right hand and most of the thumb and two fingers of the left hand. One finger of the left hand remains as good as ever and the fourth remains except the tip. All the toes on the left foot were amputated and a portion of each of the toes of the right foot."

For those interested in cold facts about the history of Longs Peak, January 12, 1925, can be remembered as the date of the "First ascent of the East Face in winter by Walter Kiener and Agnes Vaille."
[January 12, 1983]

Radioitis Epidemic Hits Estes

"The worst epidemic ever known in the history of the Estes Park territory, according to the memory of its oldest inhabitants, is now raging here. The worst features of the situation are that no known sure treatment has been discovered and the doctor himself is in the throes of the disease in its most malignant stage."

So begins an editorial in the *Estes Park Trail* of January 19, 1923. From all indications the entire area would be wiped out from a germ first discovered in 1895, amplified in ensuing years, and transmitted broadly in 1920.

The editorial continues: "The disease fastens its hold on its victim almost without warning and its presence is first manifest in the victim by a nervousness that grows as the hour approaches to close the office for the day. The victim seizes his hat and coat, jams the former well down over his ears and eyes, makes a break for home, and is just buttoning his overcoat as he strides into the house. He then plunges into a maze of diagrams, wires, spools, and coils. A few mornings later a tired appearance and bloodshot eyes indicate the victim has reached the final stages of radioitis and he finds it is necessary during the dreary and long hours at the office to prop open his eyelids with toothpicks."

Yes, Marconi discovered radio in 1895, and radio transmission of human speech was made in 1900.

Related inventions included the amplifier in 1907, heterodyne and cascade tuning receivers in 1913, and the crystal oscillator in 1918.

The first regular licensed radio broadcasting began August 20, 1920; less than two and a half years before the above editorial was written.

Estes Park claimed to have "one of the largest, if not the largest number of radio fans of any village of its size in the entire country."

There was a Rocky Mountain National Park Radio Club, whose membership was made up of those who lived in Estes Park and owned receiving sets. They also offered associate memberships to "those who are readers of the *Estes Park Trail* who have sets and are interested in the Rocky Mountain National Park region.

"...There are no fees or dues of any kind, neither are there any initiation fees. The only requirements for membership in the club are that you own a receiving set, and that you read the *Estes Park Trail.*"

The active members of the club were: Dr. Roy Wiest, Charles Chapman, Roland Reed, J.F. Schwartz, Baldpate Inn-Mace Bros., Marshal Stith, Lee Tallant, Wm. Tallant, J.F. Liebman, Electric Shop, Lewiston Hotel-A.D. Lewis, John Sherman, L.E. Osborn, Winslow Shepherd, Albert Lacook, A.K. Holmes, Ed Andrews, Julian Hayden, C.N. Rockwell, Bert Brinkley, Harry Berkley, Ray Geister, Estes Park Public Schools.

The *Trail* also published the weekly program of the Palmer School of Chiropractic Station WOC of Davenport, Iowa, "which operates one of the finest sending stations in the country."

Every day but Sunday the broadcast day began at

10:05 a.m. (mountain standard time) with opening market quotations, at 11 a.m. there was a noon chimes concert, 1 p.m.—closing stocks and markets, 2:30 p.m.—an educational talk, 4:45 p.m.—another chimes concert, 5:35 p.m.—Sandman's visit, 6 p.m.—musical program, and 7 p.m.—a lecture.

Sunday began at 8 a.m. with a sacred chimes concert, 12:45 had an orchestra concert, 5 p.m.—pipe organ concert, 5:30 p.m.—sports news, 6 p.m.—church service, and then a two-hour musical program which started at 7 p.m.

Some of the educational lectures included: Interior Decorating, How Photo Engravings Are Made, National Defense, Good Citizenship, Some Social Factors of Education, City Zoning, Margarine as a Pure and Wholesome Food, The Washing Machine as a Household Appliance, Planning and Constructing a Home, The Aloha-Land, and many others.

Saturday nights usually ended with a dance program beginning at 8 p.m.

Those early days of radio were fascinating to many people, and it is no wonder that many in the Estes Park area were victims of the "radioitis epidemic."

An example of one severe case is relayed in the January 26 *Trail:* "Charles Chapman has just recently completed a four tube radio receiving set, giving him a wide range of amplification that is working beautifully and with it he has been able to get sending stations in many parts of Canada and as far east as Cranston, Rhode Island, where he connected easily with station WKAP.

"Tuesday night the Los Angeles Times station and the

Earl C. Anthony station at the same place, stations KHJ and KFI respectively, conducted an interesting experiment. Both stations are 500 volt and KHJ was sending on 420 meters while KFI was in operation on 440 meters, or just twenty meters apart. Mr. Chapman had no difficulty in tuning out the one and the other at will so that there was absolutely no interference. The test was being made for the guidance of future legislation governing broadcasting stations. At the same time these two stations were broadcasting in Los Angeles, Mr. Chapman tuned down to 400 meters and got the Kansas City Star, WDAF, without interference from either of the others. This test would indicate that it is possible to operate stations with only a short distance in wavelength apart.

"Mr. Chapman has an interesting apparatus in connection with his home-made set. He experimented with a phonograph horn from one of the old style machines by placing it on one half of the headset. This gave good results. Later he made a Y connection so that he could connect the horn with both halves of the headset and now has an amplifier that makes concerts easily heard in all parts of the house, even through several closed doors.

"There are a number of other homemade sets in successful operation in the Park. It has been found that the crystal sets are of no value in the mountains, but the tube detector sets work very satisfactorily."

Though severely affected, Mr. Chapman and the others survived radioitis.
[January 18, 1984]

Olympic Jumper Hometown Hero

The headline across the top of the January 22, 1932, *Estes Park Trail* clearly expressed the local pride in one of our own: "Billings Places on U.S. Olympic Team at Lake Placid."

Norton Billings was not alone as a recipient of Estes Park pride, and Estes Park was not alone in being proud.

The article tells us that "The entire State of Colorado rejoiced with Estes Park region on Tuesday afternoon when telegrams came from Ted Jelema and Norton Billings at Lake Placid, N.Y., announcing the fact that Billings had 'made' the United States team for the Olympic games—held every four years to determine who's who in the cream of the cream of the world's athletes.

"...The region's entries at the jumping try-outs held at Canton, S.D., placed sixth (John Steele) and ninth (Glen Armstrong) in a field of 20 of the best ski-riders in the United States during the first half of the competitive tests held on Sunday."

Then on February 12 we see that "The National Olympics council has advanced John Steele, Estes Park jumper, from the position of alternate on the United States ski team to a place on the first team of the nation at Lake Placid, N.Y.

"Local enthusiasts have watched closely the positions of Steele and Norton Billings, the Park's cross-country entry.

"Billings was successful in making the first team at once after his arrival at the Eastern sports resort, but Steele was named an alternate first.

"News of the advance in position has given tremendous impetus to the enthusiasm for local competitors in Estes Park. The village eagerly awaits news from the Winter Sports Olympics and every person in the region is 'pulling' for Steele and Billings."

They may have all been pulling for the local contestants, but evidently not everyone appreciated their efforts.

I don't know how they placed in the world-wide competition, but the following editorial appeared on February 19: "Recently we heard someone make a disparaging statement about the small part our ski competitors played in our Winter Olympics at Lake Placid.

"Only ignorance could dictate such a statement, for few persons here had any idea that our men could either win, place, or show against the cream of the world's ski men—men who ski for a living and who were born with a pair of skis clamped to their pedal extremities, although that sounds a little difficult.

"It was wonderful enough that John Steele and Norton Billings could defeat all but a few men in the vast United States and thereby gain a place for themselves on the national team and a place for their home town in the blinding light of international publicity.

"More persons in the East and in the rest of the world have heard of Estes Park and the Rocky Mountain National Park ski club through their efforts than through any other single agency, we venture to assert, and nothing we natives can do will be too good for them when they return:"

They were certainly good, or they would not have reached the heights to compete with the "cream of the cream."

How did they get so good?

Usually it is a combination of natural talent, good coaching, and LOTS of practice:

Let's back up eight years to this week in our history.

On January 22, 1924 Cesar Tschudin arrived in Estes Park. He was a "Swiss winter sports instructor employed by the Outing Committee of the Estes Park Group of the Colorado Mountain Club to assist in the winter sports season in the Park."

He immediately organized four classes for ski instruction: young boys, high school age boys, girls, and adults. The January 25 *Trail* states:

"He is well pleased with the material he finds here among the young people and feels confident he will be able to develop several who will later give good accounts of themselves."

The *Trail* of February 29, 1924 reports, "Arriving at Hot Sulphur Springs just a few minutes after the cross country race was scheduled, Norton Billings and Barney Laycook entered the race, without a rest or dinner following a 16-mile trip on skis from Grand Lake to Hot Sulphur Springs.

"Norton Billings took second and Barney Laycook took third. Norton lost first by about three seconds in time. Had the boys had something to eat and a few moments to rest before entering the race they would likely have taken first and second respectively.

"The boys have been skiing less than two months and Estes Park is proud of their performance. "

In early March of 1924 Mr. Tschudin wrote of a ski trip from Estes Park to Grand Lake over Flat Top.

Billings and Laycook went along, so they had lots of practice before the above-mentioned race.

On March 15, 1924, Estes Park's first annual ski tournament began.

In boy's jumping, Class A, over 16, Norton Billings was third. He came in first in the men's cross country race.

The next day, in the long-standing jump, Colorado amateurs, Class B, "Norton Billings was third with 40 points, being unfortunate in breaking his skis on the first jump and therefore being unable to stand after any jump."

Seems to me that is the stuff champions are made of, whether they bring home the gold, or not.
[January 25, 1984]

Enos Mills: Father of Rocky Mountain National Park

"In the summer of 1891, while with a survey party in the Yellowstone National Park, we visited the northeast corner of that wonderland. Here I one day wandered into a romantic and park-like region that reminded me of my home by Longs Peak. 'Why not a national park of the Longs Peak region?' I at once asked myself."

The above quotation from *The Rocky Mountain National Park* tells how a spark landed on that book's author.

That spark did not die out but smoldered within Enos Abijah Mills for eighteen years before bursting into an inferno. Six years of controversy created the bellows that kept the forge working, and during this week in our history a national park was wrought.

Enos Mills was born April 22, 1870 near Fort Scott, Kansas, and came to Colorado alone when he was fourteen years old.

The next year he made the first of his 296 ascents of Longs Peak and began building a cabin across from Elkanah Lamb's Longs Peak House.

Mills bought books and studied them. He traveled and studied the places he went. He hiked and climbed and camped and studied the environment around him.

To earn a living, he worked in the Anaconda Mine at Butte, Montana, and learned while he earned, usually returning to his cabin at Longs Peak in the summer.

In 1889, Enos Mills went to California, and there he met the naturalist John Muir. Muir's inspiration and encouragement helped Enos see the knot to tie his learning experiences together.

This nineteen-year-old was on his way to becoming a naturalist interpreter, a guide who could show and explain the beauty of nature and the nature of that beauty.

Mills bought Longs Peak Inn (formerly House) from Lamb in 1902, and it became a headquarters for his conservation talks, nature tours, Longs Peak climbs, and a place for people of prominence and influence to become acquainted and hear his views.

The wording of the following quote from *The Rocky Mountain National Park* gives an Enos Mills view as well as park policy: "In these scenes the trees are never cut, the axeman is excluded. Cattle do not trample the grass and flowers. The wild deer roam free and the wild birds sing in peace. No shot is ever heard, the hunter is excluded."

In 1907, Mills was appointed by President Theodore Roosevelt to the Forest Service as an independent lecturer, and for the next two years he traveled and spoke for conservation.

The Forest Service administered the Longs Peak area as part of the Medicine Bow Range, later Colorado National Forest, and now Roosevelt National Forest. The Chief Forester was H.N. Wheeler, and both he and the Forest Service favored a game refuge over a national park in the Estes Park area.

In 1909, Enos Mills quit the Forest Service and took

up the fight for a national park.

He went on speaking tours throughout the country, continued writing in books, magazines, and newspapers, and began to gain important allies.

In April 1912, the Colorado Mountain Club was founded by Denver attorney James Grafton Rogers. They supported the creation of a national park, and Morrison Shafroth was appointed chairman of a National Park Committee.

The Colorado Mountain Club drew the first outline of the Park's boundaries and drafted each of the Park bills introduced in Congress.

In 1913 and 1914, many more organizations began to support a Rocky Mountain National Park.

Toward the end of 1914, the Rocky Mountain National Park bill was presented for a third time. The Senate version of the bill went to the House Committee on Public Lands on October 9, 1914, and did not surface again until January 12, 1915. Congress passed a slightly amended bill on the 18th, and the next day the Senate approved that amendment.

After almost six years of constant campaigning, Enos Mills had made some friends, made some foes, and become somewhat distrustful of both friend and foe. When President Woodrow Wilson signed the bill on January 26, 1915, he became something else: The Father of Rocky Mountain National Park.

[January 26, 1983]

FEBRUARY

Canyon Highway History

During the waning days of 1982 the United States Congress passed a bill that included a five cent per gallon gasoline tax: The stated purpose of that tax is to improve roads and bridges, and a spin-off would be the employment of people to do the work.

Is it a cliché or a fact that "history repeats itself?" It was during this week of our history in 1934 that the Northern Colorado Road Association was reorganized and drew up the following resolution:

"WHEREAS the Thompson Canyon Road in Larimer County, Colorado, is the most important and scenic approach to Rocky Mountain National Park, and has been approved as a Federal Aid Road and has had federal funds expended upon it but is still incomplete over the most scenic but dangerous section; and

WHEREAS the State Legislature of Colorado has made a bona fide attempt to match federal funds for the completion of this project but the legislative enactment therefore has been declared unconstitutional by the Supreme Court of the State of Colorado and it is now impossible to complete this road as a Federal Aid Project; and

WHEREAS plans and designs for the completion of this road have been prepared and are now available from the State Highway Department of Colorado so that work can be started immediately on this project giving

February

employment to a large number of unemployed men conservatively estimated at from five hundred to one thousand persons.

NOW THEREFORE BE IT RESOLVED by the Northern Colorado Highway Association composed of duly accredited and authorized representatives of the Chambers of Commerce of Estes Park, Loveland, Fort Collins, and Greeley, Colorado, that the Federal Emergency Administrator of Public Works designate the completion of this road as a Public Works Project and that sufficient funds for the completion of such Project be appropriated immediately therefore and that said Project be undertaken at the earliest possible date.

BE IT FURTHER RESOLVED that a copy of this Resolution be forwarded to the Honorable Harold S. Ickes, Administrator of the Federal Emergency Administration of Public Works at Washington, D.C., and a copy forwarded to the Senators and Representatives from Colorado in the National Congress."

It was almost a year later when the *Estes Park Trail* reported on January 25, 1935, that construction had started "...on a four mile detour around the lower part of the Big Thompson Canyon road in order to not delay traffic during the construction of one and a fifth miles of road between the Dam Store and the concrete bridge."

In the meantime, Governor Ed Johnson had outlined a plan to borrow $21 million from the Federal Government and to receive a grant of $9 million. This $30 million would enable Colorado to have a paved major road system within two years instead of the ten to fifteen years that would be required using yearly revenue. The "Committee of 63," which consisted of one representative from each county in the state, unanimously recommended adoption of the Governor's plan.

Joe Mills, Enos' brother, was Larimer County's representative and a member of the executive committee.

He stated that this plan would absorb much of the state unemployment and would not require any extra taxes. "The money would be paid back out of 70 per cent of the two-cent gasoline tax used for road construction..."

Interest on the $21 million loan would be covered by the $9 million grant.

The Committee of 63 also unanimously agreed that labor should be allotted to counties on the basis of population, with the state in control of labor assignments.

Estes Park was entitled to ten percent of the jobs on the Big Thompson project, and on January 30, Scott McGrew, Harold Rush, Howard Ray, and jackhammer operators Ralph Petit and H.F. Marsh reported for work. These five men filled the quota for the time being.

The February 8 *Trail* reported that on Friday, February 1, 1935, another day in our week in history, a lever was pushed at about 10 a.m., "...and with hardly more than a jarring sound hundreds of tons of red granite heaved slightly and then bulged down over the old road at the mouth of the Big Thompson. The sharp narrow turn by the dam will no longer give such fright to first-time tourists that their entire trip up the canyon is thereby spoiled—it is no more."

Do these events somewhat parallel history in the making almost fifty years later?
[February 2, 1983]

Estes Park's Irish Land Baron

February 12, 1841, Abraham Lincoln's 32nd birthday, marked the birth of one not quite so dear to the hearts of Estes Park's settlers as "Honest Abe."

It was in Ireland, between Limerick and Killarney, at Adare in County Limerick, that Windham Thomas Wyndham-Quin entered the world.

In 1850 the grandfather of young Thomas Wyndham died, and his father inherited a house that had been under construction for twenty years.

It was actually more than a house that Charles Edwin inherited; he also received a title. The Third Earl of Dunraven moved his family into Adare Manor—a house in which one of the rooms was 132 feet long.

Construction continued until 1862, the year Thomas Wyndham, or Lord Adare, came of age. In 1871 his father died, and he became the Fourth Earl of Dunraven.

In the meantime, he graduated from Christ Church College, Oxford, was a special correspondent for the *London Daily Telegraph* in the Abyssinian war, went with the German Army and wrote a series of articles regarding the siege of Paris, was married, and made a trip to the United States on his honeymoon in 1869.

After his father died, Lord Dunraven crossed the Atlantic again, and Christmas 1872 found him in Denver, where he heard about Estes Park. On December 27 he was here.

The hunting was superb, the beauty magnificent. The climate was invigorating and the entire area was practically uninhabited.

He returned in 1873, and in 1874 decided that he should have all of Estes Park as a private hunting preserve exclusively for the use and pleasure of his friends and himself.

After all, hadn't he grown up in a house with a 132-foot-long room in it? Didn't he inherit 40,000 acres of land and several homes including Adare Manor, Dunraven Castle at Glamorgan, Kenry House, and a town house in London?

Why shouldn't he use his wealth to preserve this wild and wonderful paradise in the mountains? He could control its development and protect it from the destruction that would surely come with civilization.

He hired Theodore Whyte to acquire the Park for him.

Men were hired from the streets and bars of Denver, Boulder, and Longmont to file claims on 160-acre parcels along the waterways of Estes Park. In attempts to satisfy legal requirements, four logs were often laid in a square and called the foundation of a cabin.

Each man hired to turn over his claim to the Earl was paid ten to fifty dollars, and the government was paid $1.25 for each acre. Conservative estimates of the Earl's acquisitions are usually stated at 6,000 acres.

In Volume I of his *Past and Pastimes,* the Earl of Dunraven states, "We pre-empted and bought land along the water, and, commanding the water, had a great area of splendid grazing country, and we put in cattle." He claimed 15,000 acres.

Whyte's men annoyed, intimidated, and discouraged

legitimate homesteaders by driving cattle onto their property, fencing off the roads to their homes, and being generally obnoxious.

From 1874 to the late 1880s, the Earl was an annual visitor, along with many relatives and friends. In 1877 he built a cottage for himself and a hotel for his friends.

Albert Bierstadt, the artist, was brought in to help choose the hotel site.

More homesteaders came, legal battles ensued with A.Q. MacGregor in the front lines, more tourists came, the hunting preserve idea was abandoned, the cattle venture failed.

Dunraven later wrote, "People came in disputing claims, kicking up rows; exorbitant land prices got into arrears; we were in constant litigation ...So we sold for what we could get and cleared out, and I have never been there since ...But I would love to see again the place I knew so well in its primeval state."

After he left in the 1880s, Lord Dunraven served in Lord Salisbury's administration as Undersecretary of the Colonies for Queen Victoria, served in the Boer War, competed for America's Cup in 1893 and 1895 with his yachts Valkyrie I and Valkyrie II, won the King's Cup in 1905, 1912, and 1921. He used his yacht as a hospital ship in World War I.

Unfortunately, his yacht Valkyrie I collided with the Santanita in the summer of 1894. It sank in about four minutes with everything on board, including Lord Dunraven's diary.

His 6,000 acres in Estes Park were purchased in 1907 by B.D. Sanborn of Greeley and F.O. Stanley of Estes Park and Newton, Massachusetts.

February 31

The English, or Estes Park, Hotel burned down on August 4, 1911, but Dunraven Cottage still stands, on private property, just off Fish Creek Road.

The Fourth Earl of Dunraven died in 1926 at the age of 85.
[February 9, 1983]

Estes Park: Ski Mecca?

"Colorado Wins National Ski Tournament for 1927"

So states the top headline on the front page of the February 15, 1926, *Estes Park Trail*.

The entire front page and a good bit of page 12 of that edition chronicled the news that the tournament would immediately follow the National Stock Show held in Denver.

A strong Colorado delegation to the National Ski Association convention and tournament being held at Duluth, Minnesota had successfully persuaded that group to come to Colorado the next year.

The following tribute is quoted in one of the articles: "Among the individuals who probably deserve especial mention for their assistance are Frank A. Bare of the Tourist Bureau, J.B. Smith, Martin Rowley, Roe Emery, A.D. Lewis and President Frank J. Habere [sic – Haberl] of the Estes Park Club."

You may want to remember the next quote from that edition: "Another factor in the selection of Colorado for the National Tournament, which is the first ever to be held in the West, was the exceedingly mild climate of the state along with the fact that there will be plenty of snow for the events."

Almost a year later, a week after the new calendar was hung, a short article appeared in the *Trail*.

It announced that the national ski meet would be

held on Saturday and Sunday, February 5 and 6, at the Genesee Course.

It also stated, "The Estes Park Club has succeeded in securing Saturday and Sunday, February 12 and 13, for the local meet and at which all the national riders taking part in Denver will attend our tournament..."

On January 21 another short article mentioned the upcoming event.

The February 4, 1927, *Trail* had the following short article. "Recently a Loveland paper carried the story of someone picking a dandelion flower in their front yard in January. Estes Park has not reported a big crop of the pretty golden flower as yet, but for several weeks the pussy willows have been out in profusion and enjoying the bright warm Estes Park January sunshine."

That same issue tells us that "The Denver Ski Club is doing everything in its power to make the national meet on February 5th and 6th a success."

As we approach this week in our history in 1927, we read in the February 11 *Trail*: "Estes Park ski fans have been scanning the skies anxiously for many days for the faintest indication that there might be a snowstorm just around the corner and that it might arrive in time to enable them to stage the scheduled ski tournament with jumpers here from all parts of the United States."

Either I missed it, or there was nothing in the *Trail* the following week to say how the tournament, so broadly heralded a year earlier, had come out.

There was something, however, that meant a great deal to many Estes Park young people during this week in our history, 1927.

The February 18 *Trail* gave the results of the School

Age Ski Tournament, sponsored by the Rocky Mountain National Park Ski Club, and held on the Deer Ridge ski course.

The following are the winners in the events:

Jumping
- Class A (boys 15 years and over): 1st, Russell Walker; 2nd, John McGraw; 3rd, Jean Byerly.
- Class B (boys 10–14 years); 1st, Fred Clatworthy Jr.; 2nd, Theodore Holmes; 3rd, Junior Duncan.
- Class B (girls 10–14 years): 1st, Martha Finn; 2nd Ruth Byerly.

Cross Country Race
- Class A (boys 15 years and over): 1st, Russell Walker; 2nd, Edward Banks; 3rd, John McGraw.
- Class B (boys 10–14 years): 1st, Merl Hurd; 2nd, Fred Clatworthy Jr.; 3rd, Calvin Finn.
- Class A (girls 15 years and over): 1st, Wilma Baldridge; 2nd, Ema Piltz; 3rd, Elsie Schwilke.
- Class B (girls 10–14 years): 1st, Ruth Byerly; 2nd, Martha Finn.
- Miss L. Worrell won the first prize in the cross-country race for the school teachers.

The article also states, "Much of the success of the tournament was due to the kindness of Ranger and Mrs. Moomaw who opened to the skiers a dining room and everyone found the noon meal most pleasant."

Did they really need the National?
[February 16, 1983]

Estes Park's Firstborn Arrived in 6th Year of Local Settlement

In Virginia, on July 6, 1806, a daughter was born to a Methodist minister and his wife, Jacob and Sarah Stollings.

A few weeks earlier, on May 25, 1806, Peter and Esther Estes had become the proud parents of a fine, strong boy in Madison County, Kentucky.

Both families migrated west, and twenty years later in Clinton County, Missouri, on November 12, 1826, twenty-year-old Joel Estes married twenty-year-old Martha Ann, or "Patsey," Stollings.

In 1833, after Patsey had given birth to the first four of thirteen children, with the fifth on the way, Joel, with his father and about 70 others, went on a prospecting, trapping, and trading trip to Santa Fe. They then went north up the front range of the Rockies to Fort Laramie before returning home from their two-year trip.

There is no record of further trips by Joel for the next thirteen years, and the last of the Estes children, Joel, Jr., was born in 1848. Let's make special mention here that the ninth, Milton, was born March 28, 1840.

By 1849, Joel and his son Hardin had gone to the California gold fields, where they reportedly found a rich vein and sold it for $30,000. Joel went home in 1850.

Joel and Hardin went back over the Oregon Trail to Baker City in 1855, then back to Missouri. Hardin eventually settled back in Baker City, Oregon.

In 1858, the year "PIKES PEAK OR BUST" was the cry after Colorado gold discoveries, Milton Estes was on the Oregon Trail and carved his name on Register Cliff, and again in 1859.

By now the oldest Estes children were married, Joel was restless again, and gold was in Colorado. Tensions were rising in Missouri with thoughts of a civil war.

This time Patsey and the youngest children went along. So did other friends and relatives, as they moved across the prairie to arrive at Auraria, Kansas Territory (now Denver) on June 15, 1859. They went to Clear Creek, near Golden, but it was over-crowded, and they then went northwest along the Platte to near St. Vrain's Fort.

Estes staked out two claims and the family "settled" again. Milton joined them.

Now let's switch to Pennsylvania, where George Archibald Fleming was born in 1816, and where the following year, on April 13, little Margaret was born to Hue and May Gordon;

By 1859 the Fleming family had moved to Galena Illinois.

Ada Belle, the third child of George and Margaret Fleming, wrote in the early 1930s, "My father, George Archibald Fleming, had crossed the Great American Desert in the spring of 1859. Liking the climate and seeking new fields, (he always had the pioneer spirit), he returned to Leavenworth, Kansas, and wrote my mother living in Galena, Illinois, to sell the house and join him in Leavenworth, for the trip West."

They left Leavenworth July 12, 1860, and arrived in

Denver August 12 in a covered wagon with six mules, a riding pony, and a "nice stock of provisions or eatables." Two weeks later, two freight wagons with supplies and equipment purchased by Fleming in Leavenworth arrived.

"In the meantime father met Joel Estes, who was holding two claims ... Father traded a yolk of oxen when they arrived and a plow and some other necessities for Mr. Estes's St. Vrain Ranch."

Before the Flemings arrived, Joel and at least one of his sons (Milton, Wesley Jasper, Francis Marion, and/or Joel, Jr.) went on a hunting and prospecting trip to the mountains.

Milton later wrote: "About the 15th of October, 1859, Joel Estes, Sr., with his son Milton... discovered what is now known as Estes Park...

"By 1863 father and I had made sufficient preparations to move our families to the Park. Father's family then consisted of my brothers, Jasper, F.M. (Marion), Joel, Jr., sister Sarah and my mother. My family, my wife and two little sons; for in the meantime I had married Miss Mary L. Fleming of St. Vrains. We were the first couple to be married in that part of the country. The first white child born in the Park was our third son, Charles F. Estes, on February 19, 1865."

Yes, neighbors being neighborly, as neighbors will— Milton Estes and Mary Louise Fleming were married on the 11th of August, 1861. They immediately moved back to Missouri where Newton was born in 1862 and George in 1863. They returned to Colorado, and during this week in our history Charles Francis Estes became the first recorded birth in Estes Park.

In 1866, after a couple of rough winters, the Estes family moved out of the Park that had been named for them. Wesley Jasper, Sarah and Francis Marion went to Iowa. Joel and Patsey, with Joel, Jr., and Milton and his family, went south through New Mexico and Texas to Arkansas, later moving back to New Mexico.

What happened to the immediate subjects of this week in our history?

The father and mother, Milton and Mary Louise, settled east of Longmont on the St. Vrain in Weld County in 1888. They later moved to Denver, where Mary Louise died in 1905. Milton died in Los Angeles in 1913.

Charles Francis, the first white child born in Estes Park, married Minnie M. Mathews of St. Vrain, Colorado, at her mother's home on January 2, 1889. They had a daughter, Ida, who died in 1912.

Charles spent most of his life working on ranches as a cowboy, or in related work with horses, etc. He was also a fireman in Boulder for a while.

Charles Francis Estes died in Boulder on October 7, 1940, and is buried in Mountain View Cemetery in Longmont, Colorado—less than forty miles from his birthplace.

[February 22, 1984]

MARCH

Estes Park Fire Gear Didn't Come Easy

The *Estes Park Trail*, on March 3, 1922, reported on a meeting held the previous Saturday night at the Odd Fellows hall. About a hundred men attended to discuss what fire protection would be best for the community.

A representative of the White Automobile Co. was there to give information and answer technical questions.

"It was the unanimous opinion of the meeting that the best possible fire fighting apparatus should be at once provided."

The Town, incorporated less than five years earlier, had a fire cart that could be taken to the scene of a fire by a Transportation Company truck and an extremely efficient crew of volunteer "Fire Laddies" to man it.

The proposal was for a fire truck with two chemical tanks, chemical hose, able to "...carry ladders and 1,000 feet of hose, axes, helmets, and the full complement of men to fight fires." It would have the power and speed to effectively protect "all parts of Estes and Rocky Mountain National Park."

The estimated cost for the truck with necessary equipment, and a building to house it, was about $10,000.

So that protection could be given to those outside the corporate limits of the Town, it was recommended that surrounding property owners contribute a third of the cost in lieu of taxes.

The proceedings of the next town council meeting were reported in the March 17th *Trail*. At that meeting the purchase of a fire truck was assured with $8,000 from taxation, provided $4,000 could be raised outside the town limits.

They stated that the tax levy would not be increased, but merely held at its present levy for three years. With the purchase of the new fire equipment the insurance rates would decrease about as much as the amount needed in taxes to pay for it.

There is no doubt that the need existed. There is no doubt that the logic of filling that need with savings of reduced insurance rates was sound.

So, it is not surprising that after a front-page appeal in the March 24 *Trail*, we see a headline the following week that states, "Fire Department Receiving Splendid Encouragement."

That encouragement is told in this paragraph: "The Fire Company hopes to install an electric siren with a range of four miles to sound alarms. So hopeful are they of the successful consummation of their efforts toward securing the truck, that they are hard at work on the tentative plans for the fire house."

Then nothing, for almost a year.

On February 5, 1923, "...fourteen of Estes Park's faithful firemen met and elected officers for the ensuing year and further determined to finish the job of raising funds to purchase a fire truck or know the reason why it can't be done."

About six hundred dollars had been raised to date.

The results of that election are as follows: Chief,

Harry W. Berkley; Assistant Chief, Frank Bond; Secretary-Treasurer, George W. Patterson; President, A.K. Holmes.

A committee consisting of Harry W. Berkley, A.B. Harris, A.K. Holmes, V.D. Hurrell, and Robert Lindley was appointed to canvass all the residents of the Park, and H. W. Berkley, C.N. Rockwell, and A. Schwilke were appointed as a committee "to straighten up the books of the company before they are turned over to the new officers."

On March 2, this week in our history 1923, the cover of the *Estes Park Trail* was printed in red and featured a photograph of a fireman fighting a spectacular blaze. The back page was also in red with a story about fires, editorially written, giving the title of the front-page photo: "'Loss Fully Covered by Insurance'—But the Business is Dead," listing the contributors to date, and giving the following reminder, "If your name is not on this list, attend to the matter before you forget it."

By April 20 they were within $300 of the goal, and the Town Council, at its April 24 meeting, ordered plans drawn for a fire house and prepared to receive bids from various truck makers.

At the May 15 meeting the City Fathers placed an order for a "...15-45 standard White fire truck, except that it will be equipped with two thirty-five gallon chemical tanks instead of one.

"The truck will be painted a brilliant red with lettering in gold, and will carry the standard fire-fighting equipment complete."

It seems the fire burned hot for a short while, died back and smoldered for almost a year, was fanned with new enthusiasm, melted the opposition, and welded together those who saw a need and answered it.

The new fire truck was delivered in August, and on September 11, 1923, it was initiated when fire was discovered on the roof of the main building at the Elkhorn Lodge. The blaze was under control in less than fifteen minutes after the alarm was received.
[March 2, 1983]

Estes Park's Notable Women

What has happened during this week in our history that has involved women associated with the Estes Park area?

Many, many things happen each week, but let's look at a few reports gleaned from a quick scan of some *Estes Park Trails* issued over 40 years ago.

In 1923 a lady involved in a great amount of Estes Park history died.

"Funeral services for Mrs. Ann Mills, mother of Joe Mills and the late Enos A. Mills, Colorado naturalist, who died Sunday of influenza after an illness of a week at her home in Pleasanton, Kan., were held there Tuesday," the newspaper reported.

"...Mrs. Mills accompanied her husband to Colorado in 1859, making the trip to Denver in a wagon during the gold rush. They returned to Kansas after a season of unsuccessful prospecting in the Colorado Rockies. Her husband, Enos Mills Sr., died 15 years ago. "Surviving Mrs. Mills are two daughters, Mrs. Ella M. Hart of Goodland, Mo., and Mrs. Wasson of Phoenix, Ariz., and two sons, Joe Mills of Estes Park and Horace G. Mills of Wages, Colo."

Then in 1927—"Mrs. Josephine Hupp was up from Loveland the first of the week arranging for the opening of the Josephine Hotel May 1 under her personal management.

"...Mrs. Hupp has been identified with the hotel business in the Park most of the time for many years. She first owned the Hupp Hotel, now owned by Mr. and Mrs. W.H. Derby. She later owned the Josephine and operated it for a time, selling it to the Lewiston Hotels Company, who operated it for several years.

"She later bought the Sherwood, selling it two years ago.

"Last fall she purchased back the Josephine Hotel from the Lewiston Hotels Company and will take personal charge of it upon opening for the season."

1932: "Dr. Margaret Fuller Boos, for two years acting naturalist at Rocky Mountain Park here, and well known in the village, has been signally honored by the American Geological Society which body has elected her to fellowship.

"Such honor has been gained by but six women of North America in the half century of the Society's existence, according to an account of the honor conferred in the current issue of the PEO Record," the *Trail* advised.

1934: "Judge Florence Allen of the Ohio Supreme Court, the only woman to occupy such a high position in the country, received higher honor this week under the new deal when President Roosevelt appointed her a judge in the United States circuit court of appeals, the highest position in the national judiciary under the federal supreme court.

"Estes Park basks in the light of glory reflected from the new robes of Judge Allen for she has made her summer home here for many years and has a fine cottage in Moraine Park."

Also in 1934: "The following poem written by Ruth Griffin, age 9, received honorable mention in a poetry contest sponsored by 'My Weekly Reader' No. 2 for children in grades three and four. Prizes of nature books were sent the three winners and Honor League buttons sent to those boys and girls receiving honorable mention.

"The children in the 3-4 grades are very proud of Ruth, as the contest was entered by hundreds of children throughout the United States.

Ruth's entry:

Skiing

One day I went skiing down a hill
But oh dear me I took a spill
My skis they slipped from under me,
And I was heading for a tree.
My brother laughed most fit to kill,
When I was sliding down a hill.

1935: "Among those altruistic people in the village who quietly go their way, doing good for the community and usually receiving slight recognition, is Mrs. Roy Baldwin. Wherever music is needed, she can be counted upon. Sometimes she receives a small remuneration, but more often all she gets is thanks—and occasionally even these are overlooked.

"We in Estes Park are fortunate that she is among us, and some of us receive pleasure from occasionally reminding Mrs. Baldwin that her efforts are appreciated.

That goes for 1983 as well, Hazel!

1936: "Miss Muriel L. MacGregor was one of 15 successful applicants for admission to the Colorado bar and the only woman admitted to practice by the Colorado Supreme Court last Friday. The examination was given last January.

"Miss MacGregor studied law at the University of Denver law school and won her degree from the institution. Few women have passed the examination and been admitted to the Colorado bar.

"Miss MacGregor comes from a pioneer Estes Park family and resides at present at the MacGregor Ranch northeast of Estes Park.

"Her grandparents came to Estes Park in 1872 and her grandfather built one of the first roads into the region. Her grandmother was a postmistress for the first term after a post office was established here.

"Miss MacGregor's grandfather was admitted to the Colorado bar about 1871, while Colorado was yet a territory."

The old papers had a lot of quotes and (sometimes) clever sayings. Here are a few from this week in our history:

1925: "Single women enjoy fiction more than married women. Perhaps the married ones hear too much of it."

1927: "What makes some Estes Park men sore is all of the money they would have to spend on themselves if they didn't have to give the wife some of it to run the house on."

1930: "Man cannot degrade woman without himself falling into degradation; he cannot elevate her without at the same time elevating himself."

[March 9, 1983]

Founder of Moraine Lodge Died in 1928

On April 17, 1844 at Orange (later the town of St. Joe) in DeKalb County, Indiana, Mary Imogene was born to John and Mary Bates. She was the second of six children, with an older brother and four younger sisters.

Almost 84 years later, on March 21, 1928, this week in our history, she died in the Methodist Hospital in Los Angeles, California, after having been struck by an automobile two days earlier.

What kind of life did this lady have, and what made her significant to Estes Park area history? '

When she was thirteen Mary Imogene was sent to an uncle in Milwaukee, Wisconsin. She had received all of the schooling available in the Orange School District and was now placed in the private school of O.M. Baker.

Baker later became president of the G&C Merriam Company, publishers of Webster's Dictionary. Her uncle, Duncan C. Reed, later served as U.S. Senator, so she was in good company.

Speaking of good company, while attending Prof. Baker's school she met Willard Owen Greene. Between 1854 and 1857 Greene, with two companions, had explored and trapped all the large rivers of Wisconsin from their source to the Mississippi.

In June 1860 Imogene Bates and Owen Greene were united in marriage.

At that time another Union was falling apart. In

defense of that Union, Owen Greene enlisted in the 24th Wisconsin Infantry. After he became ill with typhoid at Bowling Green, Kentucky, Imogene went through the Union lines and brought her husband back to Milwaukee.

By 1864 she became the first matron and Owen the first superintendent of the first National Soldiers' Home of the United States in Milwaukee.

Several more successful endeavors brought them prosperity, but their son later wrote "...in 1894 domestic troubles arose over other real estate projects and a reconciliation was impossible."

On May 12, 1898, to quote Imogene's diary: "I left [Chicago] at 10:30 p.m. for Greeley, Colo." On August 9, 1898 she wrote "Started for Estes Park this morning. Arrived at Lyons at noon. Had dinner and then took stage for Moraine, 28 miles through the mountains. Arrived here 6:30 p.m. Very tired. THE GRANDEST PLACE YET."

Why had she come?

On February 6, 1898 M. Imogene Greene had taken by relinquishment proceedings J. Pringle's homestead claim to 160 acres.

In 1903 Mrs. Greene obtained a patent to the land. In the meantime, she had another experience with typhoid, this time in southern Colorado. Some old Milwaukee friends, the McPhersons, were living in Rocky Ford, and were victims of a typhoid epidemic sweeping the area in 1901.

Imogene Greene went to their aid as nurse, but Mrs. McPherson and one daughter died. She stayed on for a while to help as needed.

In 1903 she married William D. McPherson of Rocky Ford.

Several quotes from various sources follow:

"For the first several years of this century the old Mrs. Greene homestead had nothing artificial on it but the homestead hut, a one-room log affair with no floor and a broken roof. Eventually Mrs. Greene reappeared and started building Moraine Lodge, which grew year after year until there were, in addition to the original two story building, a large dining hall and kitchen, many cottages, a stable, and finally the building which is now the Moraine Museum... Sometime during the history of Moraine Lodge Mrs. Greene married a nice looking old man by the name of McPherson. He served as clerk, but she remained definitely boss of the outfit. They both seemed well satisfied with the arrangement."

And,

"Mrs. McPherson, who owned Moraine Lodge, was one of the first 'natives' I remember.... Her name was Greene then, and she was a widow. It wasn't until several years later that she married the Scot, McPherson, and started really to build up the lodge."

And,

"My picture of Mrs. McPherson is that of a cross between Whistler's Mother and Carrie Nation."

I don't know where the Carrie Nation comes in, but she was called "Mother McPherson" by many people.

While living at Rocky Ford in 1903 she joined the Woman's Club and was elected president in 1908.

After spending summers in Estes Park, the McPhersons eventually became residents.

In 1912 Mrs. McPherson organized the Estes Park

Woman's Club, was elected president, and served in that capacity until 1920. From then until her death she was club Counselor.

In 1919 the McPhersons were visiting Los Angeles when Mr. McPherson died and was buried there.

Services were held in Los Angeles for "Mother McPherson" on March 29, 1928.

Mr. and Mrs. Reed Higby, her daughter and son-in-law, managed Moraine Lodge in 1928. By then, it consisted of forty buildings. The Lodge was leased by J.R. McKelvey in 1929.

The Moraine Lodge assembly hall, opened in July, 1923, is now the Moraine Visitors Center of the Rocky Mountain National Park.

[March 23, 1983]

Deaths Led to Shelter Cabin

"Since the death of Miss Agnes Vaille on Longs Peak and the death of Herbert Sortland who went in rescue of her, Supt. Roger W. Toll has had in mind the building of a shelter cabin on the Boulder Field."

So stated the *Estes Park Trail* this week in our history, 1925.

Roger Toll's cousin, Agnes Vaille, and Herbert Sortland brought the count to five deaths on or near Longs Peak since Toll had become superintendent of Rocky Mountain National Park in 1921, so he might have been considering the possibility of a shelter cabin for some time.

His plans were thorough, and some of the smallest details were considered.

He advocated not only a shelter for people, but a horse shelter as well.

Many people rode horses to Boulder Field, tied them to rocks in the open, and continued their climb.

Toll felt the cabin should be as near the Keyhole as possible, as its location should be "...at the furthest point to which horses might then be taken." So, the horse trail was extended.

His plan included continuous bunks to accommodate the most people, a curtain divider to separate men and women, even the type of bed springs, a stove for heating and cooking, the design of the stove pipe to avoid fire hazard or snow blowing in it, table size, benches, storage drawers, wood box, method of supplying wood, and many other details including a metal flag pole at least 25 feet high placed about 50 feet from the shelter to attract the lightning away from it.

"Stone and metal will be used as far as possible in the construction of the shelter, so as to reduce the temptation to use essential parts of the building for fuel."

Several sleeping bags were to be provided for survival without other heat.

"Each bag will be sewed together as a unit, and will be so heavy that there will be no temptation to remove it from the building."

A stable of 32 feet by 10 feet was also proposed.

By May of 1925 the Park Service was building a telephone line to Boulder Field.

Timberline Cabin would no longer be operated by Longs Peak Inn as part of their hotel system, so no emergency phone would be located there.

At that time it was stated that "No attempt will be made by the Park Service to maintain more than a summer service to Boulder Field."

Jack Moomaw wrote in his *Recollections of a Rocky Mountain Ranger,* however, "The first winter, patrols and repairs were made monthly.

"Sometimes the line would stay in order for a week or 10 days; sometimes it would go out before I got off the mountain.... by the fourth winter, these patrols were abandoned."

Supt. Toll included construction of the shelter cabin in his next estimate for an appropriation from Congress, and the following January Congressman Timberlake announced that it had been included in the 1926 budget for Rocky Mountain National Park.

Because of the short season and the necessity of taking all materials to the building site by horseback, the shelter cabin was not completed until the summer of 1927.

Also that summer, construction began on the stable. That 85-foot-long structure was built by seven men employed by the Park Service, under the supervision of Laurs Laursen.

Shortly after 1927, Robert Collier, Jr.'s application to provide meals and overnight accommodations at the Boulder Field Shelter Cabin was accepted by the National Park Service.

The original plan did not include a caretaker, but since everything had to be packed in to that 12,700-foot elevation, it was felt that the usefulness of the cabin would be limited without one.

Mr. Collier operated the shelter under lease from the Park Service for many years. The first year, overnight shelter was 50 cents, lodging $2 and meals were $1.25 to $1.75.

In his book, *Over Hill and Vale,* Harold Dunning tells how the cabin would fill with ice during the winter, and after 10 years the walls were so badly cracked that it was dynamited in 1937.

Jack Moomaw's *Recollections* are that "this Boulder Field is always slowly shifting. That is why the stone Boulder Field cabin cracked and had eventually to be abandoned."

The Boulder Field Shelter Cabin now blends with the Boulder Field. The mountain destroyed that stone and steel structure.

Such power deserves respect.

In 1926, the same year the Boulder Field cabin was started, a small stone shelter was constructed on the north side of the Keyhole, not far from where Agnes Vaille died.

Miss Vaille's father had it placed there in memory of his daughter and Herbert Sortland.

A bronze plate was attached to that memorial to tell the story.

We have not mentioned their story to make anyone fear the mountains, but let's repeat—such power deserves respect.

[March 16, 1983]

Happy Birthday, Abner

One of the very early settlers of Estes Park was Abner Sprague, and we are certainly indebted to him for writing of his life's experiences and of those that occurred around him.

His observations and philosophies were published on many occasions in the *Estes Park Trail*. The Colorado Historical Society's *Colorado Magazine* relayed his stories, and among others he wrote a short history of Larimer County for *Who's Who in Colorado* in 1938.

The Abner Sprague wit made his writings not only informative but entertaining as well.

A good example was written this week in our history, March 28, 1928: "Seventy-eight years ago today at 10 a.m. in the home of my grandfather on the bank of the Fox River at the town of Dundee, Illinois, I was born. It was a nice day, I remember, and my father was doing his plowing for spring seeding on our farm five miles away when he learned of my arrival. He stripped the harness from one of the span, threw on a blanket for a saddle, forgot to take off the collar, and made a Paul Revere ride that five miles.

"When I first saw him, that was before he seemed to see me, I was speechless; did I have to call that great big Lincoln-looking man father? I began to feel jealous, for I saw he had not made that swift ride just to make my acquaintance; by his actions I could see I was not first in his thoughts. I had to give a little grunt to attract his attentions from my mother before he noticed me. Strange, he knew my mother but had never seen me. I must have been a surprise, or a disappointment to him I know, by the way he looked at me. I wrinkled up my red nose, and winked at him, first with one eye and then the other and then both eyes. No use, it was not love at first sight. It never seemed to me as though he took much interest in me until I was big enough to spank; after that, I never thought him neglectful."

Yes, Abner Ervin Sprague was born in 1850, married Mary Alberta Morrison at Hickman, Nebraska in 1888, and died December 27, 1943, at Denver, Colorado. His 93 years hold many stories, but since we are commemorating his birth this week, let us stick to the early years.

When Abner was six years old the family was living in Floyd Center, Iowa, where he began his education, learning the alphabet and counting to twenty. Fractions came early, with an apple cut in half, then quarters.

The town grew, a new school was built, and a man teacher was hired to handle the "50 or 60 pupils in this one room... ranging from six and seven-year-olds to young men and women of twenty and twenty-one."

His learning suffered, and when Abner was ten years old, "...my father went to Pikes Peak and we moved that fall, to Illinois and lived on a farm with an uncle, my father's brother.

"This uncle, like most farmers in those days, thought that if there was work on the farm for boys my size, it was better to skip school and do it."

The main thing Abner learned in Illinois was that he

had had enough of farming.

In 1864, Abner, with his sister, brother, and mother, came to Colorado Territory to join his father.

Two years later the first public school in Larimer County was established, and Abner's learning flourished, mainly due to his determination and an understanding and willing teacher.

"With her I took up natural philosophy—now called physics—and algebra; she had never studied either and she was not obliged to teach them, but she was good enough to join me in their study." Abner went on to become a civil engineer, and among other things was Larimer County Surveyor for three terms.

But let us get back to his birthday. In 1930 he wrote: "Children now begin having birthday parties when they are one year old. My first birthday party was when I was 17, so you can see I had missed 16 such parties when I was 17 by being born in 1850 instead of 70 years later. But I certainly would have missed such a party as my first one in that 16x24 cabin with its dirt floor had I been born many years later."

The main feature of that party was a taffy pull, and even after their parents left to visit an uncle, Abner, his sister and six school-mates had to expand their activities outdoors part of the time. They kicked up such a dust from the floor they had to go outside to breathe, and then sprinkle the gunny sack carpet to settle the dust.

"The taffy was inclined to taste a little earthy, but not enough to spoil it... all in all, my first pioneer party was a success."

Happy Birthday, Abner!
[March 30, 1983]

APRIL

Enos Mills Promoted Conservation

During this month of our history, on April 22, 1870, a boy was born on a farm near Pleasanton, Kansas. That boy would grow up to make history and to change the course of events in the Estes Park area forever. He came to Estes Park at the age of fourteen, and the following year built a small cabin at the base of Longs Peak. From that cabin he studied and wrote. He became a self-taught naturalist, and a teacher of nature.

Enos Mills was his name, and he taught not only small groups on mountain trails, but individuals by the thousands through his writings. He authored many books and an untold number of articles as he campaigned for the preservation of nature in general and the establishment of Rocky Mountain National Park in particular.

Let's jump ahead forty-five years from his birth to April 15, 1915 when the book *The Rocky Mountain Wonderland* by Enos Mills was published by Houghton Mifflin Co. Between the time that book was written and its publishing date the Rocky Mountain National Park was established after a six-year campaign by its author. If you will allow me to quote from its pages, perhaps we can get a better feel for Enos Mills' philosophy to preserve nature for people to use, but not abuse.

The following quotes are all taken from the chapter titled "The Conservation of Scenery," which begins on

April   61

page 313.

"The comparative merits of the Alps and the Rocky Mountains are frequently discussed. [Theodore] Roosevelt and others have spoken of the Colorado Rockies as 'The Nation's Playground.' This Colorado region really is one vast natural park. The area of it is three times that of the Alps."

Also—"The climate of the Rocky Mountains is more cheerful than that of the Alps; there are more sunny days, and while the skies are as blue as in Switzerland, the air is drier and more energizing.

"But the attractions in the Alps are being preserved, while the Rocky Mountains are being stripped of their scenery. Yet in the Rocky Mountains there are many areas rich in perishable attractions which might well be reserved as parks so that their natural beauties could be kept unmarred. It is to be hoped that the growing interest in American scenery will bring this about before these wild mountain gardens are shorn of their loveliness.

"The United States is behind most nations in making profitable use of scenery. Alpine scenery annually produces upward of ten thousand dollars to the square mile, while the Rocky Mountains are being despoiled by cattle and sawmills for a few dollars a square mile...

"The unfortunate fact is that our scenery has never had a standing. To date, it has been an outcast. Often lauded as akin to the fine arts, or something sacred, commonly it is destroyed or put to base uses. Parks should no longer be used as pigpens and pastures. These base uses prevent the parks from paying their dividends in humanity."

And, "In these varied attractions of our many natural parks we have ample playgrounds for all the world and the opportunity for a travel industry many times as productive as our gold and silver mines—and more lasting, too, than they. When these scenes are ready for the traveler we shall not need to nag Americans to see America first; and Europeans, too, might start a continuous procession to these wonderlands.

"In the nature of things, the United States should have a travel industry of vast economic importance. The people of the United States are great travelers, and we have numerous and extensive scenic areas of unexcelled attractiveness, together with many of the world's greatest natural wonders and wonderlands which everyone wants to see...

"I suppose that in order to lead Americans to see America first, or to see it at all, and also to win travel from Europe, it is absolutely necessary to get America ready for the traveler. The traveler's ultimatum contains four main propositions. These are grand scenery, excellent climate, good entertainment, and swift, comfortable transportation. When all of these demands are supplied with a generous horn of plenty, then, but not until then, will multitudes travel in America...

"A park requires eternal vigilance. The better half of our scenic attractions are the perishable ones. The forests and the flowers, the birds and the animals, the luxuriant growths in the primeval wild gardens, are the poetry, the inspiration, of outdoors. Without these, how dead and desolate the mountain, the meadow, and the lake!

"...Every park is a place of refuge, a place wherein

wild life thrives and multiplies. As hunters are perpetually excluded from all parks, these places will thus become sanctuaries for our vanishing wild life. All wild life quickly loses its fear and allows itself to be readily seen in protected localities. Wild life in parks thus affords enjoyment by being readily seen, and from now on this life will become a factor in education. Children who go into parks will be pleasantly compelled to observe, delightfully incited to think, and will thus become alert and interested—will have the very foundation of education. Perhaps it is safe to predict the tendency will be to multiply the number of parks and decrease the number of zoological gardens...

"Although parks pay large dividends, they also have a higher, nobler use. They help make better men and women. Outdoor life is educational. It develops the seeing eye, supplies information, gives material for reflection, and compels thinking, which is one of the greatest of accomplishments. Exercise in the pure air of parks means health, which is the greatest of personal resources, and this in turn makes for efficiency, kindness, hopefulness, and high ideals. Recreation in parks tends to prevent wasted life by preventing disease and wrong-doing. The conservation of scenery, the use of scenic places for public recreation parks, is conservation in the highest sense, for parks make the best economic use of the territory and they also pay large dividends in humanity."

Mills also saw the necessity for separation of Forest and Park.

"Each of these serves in a distinct way, and it is of utmost importance that each be in charge of its specialist. The forester is always the lumberman, the park man is a practical poet; the forester thinks ever of lumber, the park man always of landscapes. The forester must cut trees before they are over-ripe or his crop will waste, while the park man wants the groves to become aged and picturesque... It would be folly to put a park man in charge of a forest reserve, a lumbering proposition. On the other hand, what a blunder to put a tree-cutting forester in charge of a park! We need both these men; each is important in his place; but it would be a double misfortune to put one in charge of the work of the other.

A National Park service is greatly needed."

By the time this book was published, the Secretary of the Interior had appointed a Superintendent of National Parks.

I think Enos Mills would approve of our ending this column of quotes from his book with the account of a United States Circuit Court decision in Colorado that "the beneficial use of a stream was not necessarily an agricultural, industrial, or commercial use, and that, as part of the scenery, it was being beneficially used for the general welfare. The question was whether the waters of a stream, which in the way of a lakelet and a waterfall were among the attractions of a summer resort, could be diverted to the detriment of the falls and used for power. The judge said 'No,' because the waters, as used, were contributing toward the promotion of the public health, rest and recreation; and that as an object of beauty—'just to be looked at'—they were not running in waste but were in beneficial use. He held that objects of beauty should not be destroyed because they are without assessable value.

"The judge, Robert E. Lewis, said in part: 'It is a beneficial use to the weary that they, ailing and feeble, can have the wild beauties of Nature placed at their convenient disposal. Is a piece of canvas valuable only for a tentfly, but worthless as a painting? Is a block of stone beneficially used when put into the walls of a dam, and not beneficially used when carved into a piece of statuary? Is the test dollars, or has beauty of scenery, rest, recreation, health and enjoyment something to do with it? Is there no beneficial use except that which is purely commercial?' This decision is epoch-marking."

So wrote Enos Abijah Mills in 1915.
["This Month in History," April, 1985]

Illustrating Early Estes

In 1927 a map of Rocky Mountain National Park and its surroundings suddenly appeared in the larger hotels of Estes Park, and in the studio of Fred Payne Clatsworthy.

The map was unique—Twin Sisters Mountain was shown with two blondes, Twin Owls was, naturally, two owls, and a man's head formed Old Man Mountain.

There was a picture of a man calling a bluff, "Here Cliff, Here Cliff," and many other clever illustrations covered its surface.

Altitudes, trails, roads, hotels, and inns were also there, making it a useful guide as well as a novelty.

That map introduced its creator to the Estes Park area, and the following year Mr. Richardson Rome became associated with Dave Stirling, Estes Park artist, in a gallery recently opened by Mr. Stirling.

"Dick" Rome, a student at the University of Minnesota Art Institute from 1920 to 1925, then art director for the Minneapolis office of Fawcett Publications, and now 26 years old and manager of Alden Galleries in Kansas City, Mo., was fast becoming a master of his art, etching.

He made it sound so simple when he explained the process: "First a protecting surface, called ground, is laid over a piece of copper. Then I scratch into the copper through the ground with a steel point.

"Acid is applied next and this eats into my scratched

surface, giving depth to the lines. I remove the ground and the plate is ready for printing."

In 1929 Mr. Rome moved to the Little Bond Shop on the Hill, a little log cabin on the side of the hill, just above where the Post Office was at that time in Bond Park.

The next year the name was changed to the Romeart Studio, and Dick Rome brought a collection of original etchings from Alden Galleries to display with his own works.

He also added a circulating library in which were found the most recently published novels.

Miss Elizabeth Brewster of Kansas City and formerly a Grand Lake summer resident, was in charge of Romeart for the season.

Remember that name, for on August 21, 1939 Mr. Rome married Betty Brewster of Kansas City.

But let's step back into 1933, the year Richardson Rome and Clem Yore, Estes Park author, published *High Country: An Artist's Colorado.* The limited edition of 1,050 copies, each signed by the artist, contained a group of new woodcuts by Rome and two poems, "Colorado" and "Sage of the Timberline," by Yore.

That volume was accepted for the permanent collections at the Metropolitan Museum of Art and at the Brooklyn Museum of Art, both in New York City.

The next year, a book entitled *Rocky Mountainania, or a Tenderfoot's Dictionary* made its appearance. The authors were Miss Harriet Peters, Dave Stirling, and Richardson Rome.

Miss Peters wrote the words from her experiences at Elkhorn Lodge and with tourists generally. Dave Stirling drew the cartoons and Dick Roma provided scores of woodcuts.

According to one account, "It sparkles with funny definitions. You will be delighted to see how many different kinds of jam there are and that acres are front yard measurements out west."

Also in 1934, the Romeart moved to the Clatworthy Building, which had been Estes Park's original school building. It had been moved five doors west of the Estes Park Bank.

In 1935, Mr. Rome began producing etching and woodcut postcards.

In 1937, in association with Calvin Williams, Rome Creations introduced other writing paper items featuring etchings of mountain scenes, and in 1939 the printing operations were moved to Denver with Williams in charge.

Mr. and Mrs. Rome moved to Boulder in 1941 where he established the Originals Division of Rome Creations.

In 1944 Rome and Williams opened a display and sales office in New York City for distribution throughout the United States and other countries.

Ten years later Rome Creations was phased out of operation, and Mr. and Mrs. Rome opened the Betty Brewster of Boulder shop. It featured Rome's work, yarns, and gifts.

On February 16, 1967, Betty Rome died. Dick Rome then moved to Phoenix, Arizona.

He was married there in 1968, and his second wife, Marjorie, died in September 1980.

This week in our history, on April 4, 1981, while visiting his son, Robert, and daughter-in-law in Aspen, Richardson "Dick" Rome died.

One of the many artists who has made Estes Park his home was gone at the age of 79.
[April 6, 1983]

Newspaper Life Since 1908

As previously noted, the Town of Estes Park is not very old, having been platted in 1905 and incorporated in 1917. Consequently, newspapers in Estes Park are all fairly recent, too, even in comparison to other towns and cities in Colorado.

The Park's first newspaper was *The Mountaineer*, published during the summer of 1908, with Volume I, Number 1, dated June 4. The editor was J. Gordon Smith, and the paper was published every Thursday at Estes Park, with subscription at $2.00 per year.

Then on June 15, 1912, Vol. I, No.1 of *The Estes Park Trail* appeared. It was a small booklet published every Saturday during June, July, August, and September by J.Y. Munson; with the "Principal Office" in Berthoud and the Estes Park office with W.T. Parke. Subscription was 75 cents per year or 5 cents per copy. That lasted through Volume III, or 1914.

Next came the *Estes Park Alikasai*, a semi-weekly in 1914 and 1915. I'm not sure how long it lasted, as I've only seen one copy, a pre-season issue in 1915.

The *Alikasai* was published by Mark A. Ellison and Claude H. Smith, with Fern Cramer as editor.

The *Trail Talk* came out on Fridays in 1920, with Archibald Taylor as editor and publisher. It was a small booklet like the *Trail* of earlier days, and sold for 20 cents a copy, or $1.75 a season.

April 71

That brings us up to this week in Estes Park history—April 15, 1921. That was the date printed on Vol. I, No.1 of the new *Estes Park Trail*, and the beginning of continuous publication of a newspaper in Estes Park, Colorado.

The subscription rates were: One year, cash in advance—$3.00; Six months—$1.75; Three months—$1.00; Single copy—ten cents.

The *Trail* office was in the Josephine Hotel building (The Wheel is there now), and the shop was above Clem Yore's Big Thompson Hotel in Prospect Heights.

Perhaps we can let A.B. Harris, the editor and publisher, tell you a little of how the paper got started, his hopes for its future, and a hint of his general philosophy as he did in that first editorial:

"The *Estes Park Trail* is a reality at last. Late in February it became apparent that a venture like this could be made a success. At that time there were few of the business men of the Park here; but after interviewing those who were here, we were assured the hearty support of every one of them, as is evidenced by the appearance of our advertising columns in this issue, and we decided to establish ourselves at once, well knowing there could be no doubt of the success of such an undertaking if we received the same wholehearted support from those other business men who were out of the Park for the winter. That we will have their support to the utmost has already been demonstrated although we have been unable yet to interview all of them.

"The hearty support, we may properly say the hilarious support, we have received on every hand has made our coming, brief residence here and strenuous labors in getting ready for publication, days of joy to us. To say that we appreciate your sympathy and support in this undertaking is putting it mildly, and yet we know not words that will stronger express our feeling.

"We plan to make this the very best paper it is possible for our ability plus your continuous support and co-operation to produce. It is our hope that it shall at all times favorably reflect the wonderful community in which it is published and through its columns many may be led to make the acquaintance of the Park and that many others who cannot be here the year round may through its columns keep in touch with the activities of the Park and its beauties. We trust each morning as we rise and begin our labors of joy, for such the work is to us, that we gaze upon the wonderful, the majestic handiwork of God, we may be given a fresh inspiration that may be reflected in a gladsome way. However no individual by himself can make a successful publication. Its success depends also on the readers and advertisers. There isn't an individual in the Park but that can assist us in making the paper we all would have it be by calling and imparting to us bits of information that came your way. True, a successful editor has a 'nose for news,' but aforesaid nose is not infallible nor ever present, hence we must depend largely on you for assistance in making up the paper's news columns. Do not get the mistaken idea that you are unduly pushing yourself forward by telling us what you are doing, or what your plans may be to make this a better and more attractive community in which to live.

"The policy of the paper shall be justice and fairness to all, favoritism to none. We trust that this meets with the hearty approval of all. If there are community differences we beg that you will not expect us to mix in them, except when they become moral matters. We are here to present to the world the attractive features of the community. We shall at all times try to grant the other fellow respect for his opinions and ask for ourselves the same great American right. We trust that we shall be able to respect and love you each and look for that which is manly and noble in you each, forgetting those things which are in us all, commonly known as human limitations."

A few of the news items in that first issue might also be of interest.

The top left corner of page one tells us that "There was great excitement one morning recently when employees of the Transportation Co. came down to work and found what appeared to be the tracks of a huge grizzly bear in the dust-covered courtyard of the office. The animal did no damage."

The top right corner reveals that "State Auto License Inspector Schoonmaker was in Estes Park Sunday, April 3rd, checking up on the car owners who were operating their cars without a 1921 license, as about thirty persons can testify."

On page seven we read that Mrs. Flora Manford had died on April 4th at the hospital in Longmont where she had undergone surgery for cancer.

Mrs. Manford had been a Park resident for twenty-six years and had been married to John Manford. He was the builder of the Manford House, which had been sold to Josephine Hupp and is still known as the Hupp Hotel.

An item of urban renewal appeared on page eight: "Contracts were recently let to Geo. W. Johnson for the widening of the two bridges over Fall River and the bridge over the Big Thompson at the lower entrance to the village. Heretofore these bridges have been of single and double width and with the immense amount of traffic now entering the Park during the tourist season have become far too small.

"The bridge over Fall River at the upper end of Elkhorn Ave. has been widened to almost the full width of the street. The bridge near the picture theatre has been widened so that it will permit the passing of several vehicles at the same time, and the bridge over the Big Thompson at the lower end of Elkhorn Ave. is being widened to double width."

And, if you have been concerned or disturbed about the weather this past winter, or so far this spring—take note of the following notice to subscribers that was also found on page seven.

"Because of the heavy snow, the extra duties caused thereby, the loss of telephone service, and the disablement of the power plant for three days prevented our getting the paper out on Friday, we appear three days late. We are compelled to leave out much news and print eight pages instead of twelve."

Even though Vol. I, No. 1 got off to a late start, there has been a newspaper in Estes Park at least once a week ever since.

[April 20, 1984]

How the Village Became a Town

In 1915 a Denver newspaper reported that "Estes Park is without a major, a council, a commission or anything else in the form of a governing body, yet it is a model of progressiveness."

Let's step back and take a look at some highlights of that progress.

In 1859, the Colorado Gold Rush was in full swing when Joel Estes set foot in the "park" that was to bear his name.

While miners, prospectors, and entrepreneurs of all kinds were rushing to Central City, Blackhawk, Gold Hill and other mining areas, the Estes family was settling in to hunt, fish, and raise cattle in a beautiful, peaceful valley.

The Estes family left in 1866, and within a few years was replaced by quite a number of others who had settled in the park, most with the thought of raising cattle.

Travelers came to visit the area, to view its beauty and enjoy what it had to offer.

Cattlemen became innkeepers.

Lord Dunraven came, saw, and controlled thousands of acres for many years. His private hunting preserve and cattle ranch kept the area in a somewhat natural state into the 20th century.

In 1905 C.H. Bond, J.R. Anderson, W.L. Beckfield,

and J.Y. Munson formed the Townsite Company, bought 160 acres at the confluence of the Big Thompson and Fall Rivers from John Cleave, and laid out the town of Estes Park. At that time there were only five buildings on what became Elkhorn Avenue.

The census records for Estes Park and the area south to the Boulder County line, west to the Continental Divide, about eight miles east and about ten miles north show a steady, but not extremely rapid, increase. The population was 125 in 1890, 218 in 1900, 396 in 1910, and 539 in 1920.

Quite a contrast to the boom towns in the mining area where populations increased by the thousands in days or weeks.

There were other contrasts as well—when the boom went bust the population went down as fast as it went up, and once-prosperous mining towns became ghost towns surrounded by the scars, gashes, ruptures, and disfigurements left behind by man's quest for sudden riches.

Now close your eyes and picture a rough and ready mining town on Saturday night, then read another quote from that 1915 paper—"The only official in Estes Park is a Constable, and it is freely declared that he does not know he is working.

"That applies to Estes Park at the height of the tourist season as well as in its quietest winter hours. For in some manner the atmosphere of right doing spreads to the thousands who flock through the mountain portals of Estes Park every summer."

Things were bound to change, though; 1915 was the year Rocky Mountain National Park was established, and the number of summer visitors to and through Estes Park increased tremendously.

The responsibility of the village to properly care for these people increased accordingly, and Estes Park was soon to have a government.

We don't want to leave the impression that Estes Park fumbled along and accidentally gained the reputation observed and reported by the *Denver Times* in 1915.

In 1906, C.H. Bond, with the help of Enos Mills, F.O. Stanley, and other leaders of the community formed the Estes Park Protective and Improvement Association. Stanley was the first president.

The Protective Association was a forum and meeting place where squabbles could be ironed out and resolutions for the common good were passed. In short, order without law.

On April 3, 1917 an election was held to determine if the Town of Estes Park would be incorporated. Of the ballots cast, 73 were for incorporation and 12 were against.

So in this week in our history, on April 17, 1917, Estes Park became an incorporated town.

Dr. Roy Weist was elected mayor, and Albert Hayden, E.D. Lindley, J.E. MacDonald, J.F. Schwartz, C.N. Rockwell, and A.D. Lewis were the Town's first Trustees. Charles F. Hix was appointed Clerk and Recorder.

In all due respect to the Protective Association and to your theory, Thomas Jefferson, that the least governed are the best governed, it had to happen sooner or later. [April 20, 1983]

MAY

Presbyterians and the 'Devil'

Ferdinand Vandiveer Hayden conducted U.S. Geological and Geographical surveys of Colorado and the adjacent territory in 1873, 1874, and 1875. He was in Estes Park in 1873.

At the museum we have an atlas published on completion of those surveys, in which Estes Park is clearly shown. Just north of Estes Park is Devil's Canon, shown running into Cow Creek, and then to the North Fork of the Big Thompson. (What is called Cow Creek on later maps is called So. Cow Creek by Hayden, and the "Cow Creek" mentioned above is called West Creek on later maps.)

When. Hayden's "Devil's Canon" became Devil's Gulch we do not know, but *High Country Names* by Arps and Kingery says "Devil's Canon probably changed to Devil's Gulch by popular western usage; not gorge, which word is western but derives from an old French word meaning whirlpool, nor gully which is cousin to gullet, also French, but gulch, a purely western word."

So now we have the "Gulch;" what about the "Devil's"?

Also in *High Country Names* we read, "Perhaps it earned its satanic reputation from the way the clouds boil up from it, like smoke spewing out of Hell, long after the sun has burned off the clouds on the higher slopes."

"Mountain Jim" Nugent, Lord Dunraven, and others

probably hunted in this area in the early days.

In the *History of the Big Thompson Canyon*, Mrs. Harold Easterday wrote, "One of the earliest cattle men in this locality was George W. Ragen. He ran cattle on the North Fork in the early 1870s... in the eighties, PJ. Pauley acquired extensive property in the region. He engaged in stock ranging and became owner of what is now McGraw Ranch, also Devil's Gulch Ranch."

In 1893, O.S. and Ira Knapp established a saw mill at Harding Heights, and in 1896 they moved it to Devil's Gulch, and were joined by Mason Knapp who filed claims on land in the area.

An 1897 photograph calls the area Knappsville.

Shortly after 1900 George Dennis homesteaded near the foot of Devil's Gulch and became the Road Overseer when the County took over the road from Drake to Estes Park. Dennis is credited with adding the hairpin turns to alleviate the steep grade and with improving the road so it followed the stream instead of going cross-country.

Reverend W.H. Schureman was a lay Sunday school missionary in the West, travelling from place to place organizing Sunday schools and churches.

In the summer of 1899, while in the vicinity, he heard that Mason Knapp, his friend and fellow Presbyterian from Illinois, was living in Devil's Gulch. He promptly came to visit.

In the ensuing months, they determined that Devil's Gulch would be an ideal location for a summer resort "for the Presbyterian people of Boulder Presbytery, including the pastors of its churches."

Mason and his youngest brother, Samuel P. Knapp, were in possession of most of the land wanted or needed for the proposed association. They agreed to sell the land for a nominal amount.

Over the next few years the planning of the Presbyterian Assembly Association took place, and during this week in our history, on May 3, 1903, it was incorporated.

W.H. Schureman was appointed Superintendent of the Association for 1903.

Mason Knapp agreed to $1,300 as his price for lands sold, and in August the treasurer was authorized to pay him $75 on account. He and his brother eventually received the balance due either in cash, timber, or lots.

According to Mr. Schureman's memoir, as recorded in Joseph Knapp's book, *The Glen Haven Story,* "Shares of stock were offered to purchasers at $50 per share, entitling each shareholder to a deed of a tract of ground for a cabin site 200 by 300 feet fronting on a stream, of which there were three, running through these grounds."

Mr. Schureman hated the name Devil's Gulch, considering it blasphemous and profane. His proposal of the name Glen Haven was accepted and adopted as the permanent name for the Association's holdings, and the Presbyterians were no longer in Devil's Gulch.

[May 4, 1983]

Sheriff, Realtor, Benefactor

"WHEREAS, according to the second amended plat of The Town of Estes Park, a certain block of ground designated as "Park," is now the property of The Town of Estes Park;

WHEREAS, public buildings of the Town, together with a public park, are now located on said property;

AND WHEREAS, The Town of Estes Park acquired said property by gift and donation from one C.H. Bond, now deceased, a pioneer resident and civic minded builder of this community;

NOW THEREFORE BE IT RESOLVED BY THE BOARD OF TRUSTEES OF THE TOWN OF ESTES PARK, that in order to perpetuate the memory of C.H. Bond, said block of ground is hereby dedicated to C.H. Bond, and henceforth shall be known as "BOND PARK."

(Signed) Glen H. Preston, Mayor

Attest: (signed) Vern H. Fanton, Town Clerk

The above resolution, adopted during this week in our history, states that Bond Park was dedicated "in order to perpetuate the memory of C.H. Bond."

Did we succeed in that honorable goal?

How many of us reading these lines know who C.H. Bond was, or what he did to have the focal point of downtown Estes Park named in his honor?

In all due respect to our Town Fathers, and to the *Estes Park Trail*, we didn't get off to a very good start "to perpetuate the memory of C.H. Bond." The report of the May 8 Town Board meeting that appeared in the *Trail* on May 12, 1944, somehow omitted mention of the Bond Park resolution.

We cannot give a detailed biography in these few lines, but we realize nothing is "perpetual" without an occasional boost, so here is a slight nudge.

Cornelius H. Bond was born October 9, 1854 in Guernsey County, Ohio. He attended Muskingum College, New Concord, Ohio, and headed west in 1879. He arrived in Loveland, Colorado on St. Patrick's Day.

That summer Mr. Bond and several others came to Estes Park on a camping trip. Later that year he was called back to his hometown and did not return until January 1883.

Five years later C.H. Bond and Frona Sullivan, a daughter of pioneers in the Big Thompson Valley, were married. In 1895, Mrs. Bond died in Loveland.

On May 7, 1896 Alma Sanborn became Mrs. C.H. Bond.

In the fall of 1895 Bond was nominated for the office of Larimer County Sheriff on the Republican ticket and was elected in November by the largest plurality cast to that time (1,234). He was reelected in 1898 and served for a total of five years.

During his term as Sheriff, Mr. Bond covered much of this area on horseback. He usually went on the only road at that time between Estes Park and Loveland, across Bald Mountain, but many times he followed the Big Thompson through the canyon.

May

He could foresee a highway along that beautiful river, but others could not see the road, envision the "tourists" he talked about, or any connection between the two.

In 1902, as a member of a committee to study the Bald Mountain Road, he recommended a road up the Big Thompson, and was instrumental in its completion in 1904.

In *Highlights of the History of Estes Park*, Mrs. C.H. Bond wrote, "In 1905 a company was formed in Loveland, Colorado to buy 160 acres in Estes Park from John Cleve [sic] and layout a town. The company was called the Townsite Company and consisted of C.H. Bond, J.R. Anderson, W.L. Beckfield, and J.Y. Munson.

"...In 1906, the Townsite Company put in a water system for the Town. The water was brought from a dam at the head of Black Canyon Creek. Mr. C.H. Bond had full charge of the system until 1929 when the Town took it over."

In the first plat of Estes Park in 1906 there was no park, but on the Second Amended Plat of Estes Park, dated April 7, 1908, individual lots had been removed in the block now known as Bond Park, and it was labelled "Park."

When the Post Office building was erected on the site by C.H. Bond and others, it and the ground on which it stood was donated to the Town for a Post Office and other public buildings. The library and Town Hall were later built there.

Mr. Bond, as a member of the State Legislature for three terms, helped to create the State Highway Commission.

His interest in roads carried over into the building of

Fall River Road.

He established the C.H. Bond & Co. Real Estate Agency in Estes Park, and handled the sale of F. O. Stanley's interests in 1926. That included the Stanley Hotels, Power Plant, and about 2,750 acres of land.

For several months in 1930, Mr. Bond had been confined to his home because the blood was not circulating to his right foot. It became necessary on November 29 to amputate his right foot and leg above the knee.

On May 27, 1931, Cornelius H. Bond died at his home in Estes Park, and in 1944 Bond Park was named to perpetuate his memory.

[May 11, 1983]

Music: A Timeless Attraction

"Is music just an enjoyment and a luxury? Or is it an inspiring force in the lives of people and communities?

"President Coolidge and other leaders must have thought it was something more than a mere pleasure, when they gave endorsement to National Music Week...

"When King Saul of ancient Israel lost his grip on life, they sent young David into his tent to play on the harp...

"A power that can thus influence sentiment is a force to be reckoned with in building personal and community character."

The above quote is copied from the May 23, 1924 *Estes Park Trail* and is there credited to the *Jefferson County Republican.*

Let's back up a year to a headline in the May 25, 1923, *Trail*: "THE FIRST CELEBRATION OF MUSIC WEEK IN ESTES PARK A TREMENDOUS SUCCESS."

The story goes on to tell that "The Estes Park Music and Study Club closed a most successful Music Week in Estes Park amid the praises and congratulations of appreciative audiences at each of the impressive entertainments given to the public."

The two main entertainments of that first music week in Estes Park were during this week in our history.

On May 17 about three hundred attended as the Conservatory Concert Program Artists from the Agriculture College in Ft. Collins performed at the

Stanley Casino. That group included "ten prominent singers, pianists, an exceptional violinist and a reader, Mrs. Emslie, wife of Professor A. Emslie, playing several piano accomplishments."

The May 19 entertainment filled the auditorium at the Elkhorn Lodge to capacity. That program featured local artists including Mrs. Frank Service, Miss Lois Griffith, Mrs. Clifford Higby, Mrs. A.B. Harris, Mrs. Robert Lindley, Mrs. Fred Carruthers, Mrs. F.P. Clatworthy, Mrs. Pieter Hondius, and other members of the Music and Study Club.

Sixty years later, on May 6, 1983, a headline in the *Estes Park Trail-Gazette* says, "Music Festival Begins in Estes."

The Wildflower Music Festival of 1983, from May 8 to June 13, is also during this week in our history—and before—and after.

Backing up again, let's see what happened before that first music week in Estes Park—and after.

The Estes Park Music and Study Club was organized by Alberta Yore on June 18, 1918 with the object to embrace "the study of music in all its forms; the fine arts in general, including painting, literature, sculpture and the stage and such kindred studies analogous to these..."

Mrs. Yore was the daughter of Byron Wesley McAuley, a writer and violinist from Minnesota, and wife of Clem Yore, Estes Park poet and author.

The Music and Study Club was an inspiration to many people for many years.

On July 4, 1921, the formal opening and dedication of Mountain Hall took place. Mountain Hall was the main building of the Rocky Mountain School of Music, founded by John M. Rosborough, Dean of Music at the University of Nebraska, and Arne Oldberg, Director of the piano department at Northwestern University School of Music.

"There are several plans that may be selected by the students for pursuing a course of study at their option, including any theoretical subject. Practice cottages and pianos are provided and every facility that will aid in the study of music is at hand. The regular tuition rates are $75 for the term."

In 1924 the Rocky Mountain School of Musical Art was founded in Estes Park by Mrs. Maud Biard of Waxahachie, Texas, a teacher of both piano and voice.

By transposing a couple of numbers, we quickly arrive at 1942, the year Miss Beth Miller founded the Rocky Ridge Music Center.

In 1951 Rocky Ridge purchased the Hewes-Kirkwood Inn at the foot of Longs Peak, and Beth Miller Harrod continues as director of that school for the study of music, its performance and appreciation. Music in the Mountains continues.

The year 1960 brought Dr. Walter Charles and the Blue Jeans Symphony. In 1965 the name was changed to the "Colorado Philharmonic." They later moved to Evergreen, where Dr. Charles died a few years ago.

The list goes on and on with diversity of people, music, and events. Recent history includes the Barleen Family Theater, and the establishment in 1982 of the Colorado Country Music Hall of Fame in Estes Park.

We have only touched on a few of the many musical forces "to be reckoned with in building personal and

community character." Perhaps in the weeks to come we can study them individually, but collectively Estes Park's musical heritage has helped build a "community character" seldom, if ever, equaled.
[May 18, 1983]

The Lake Slept in Silence

"From the dry, buff grass of Estes Park we turned off up a trail on the side of a pine-hung gorge, up a steep pine-clothed hill, down to a small valley, rich in fine, sun-cured hay about eighteen inches high, and enclosed by high mountains whose deepest hollow contains a lily-covered lake, fitly named 'The Lake of the Lilies.' Ah, how magical its beauty was, as it slept in silence, while there the dark pines were mirrored motionless in its pale gold, and here the great white lily cups and dark green leaves rested on amethyst-colored water."

Such is the way Isabella Bird described Lily Lake in October 1873. She was on her way to climb Longs Peak with Mountain Jim as her guide.

For almost seventy-eight years the great white lily cups and dark green leaves on amethyst-colored water "slept in silence."

About 1914, Katherine Garetson, of Big Owl Tea Place, wrote "...there dwelt a very pleasant young man, Julian Johnson. He, too, was a homesteader. Half of his claim was lovely Lily Lake. The north shore rises abruptly into a rugged little mountain whose crest resembles a cluster of Gothic church spires, while off toward the west towers the snow-capped range."

It seems that beauty begat beauty, and in 1924 the Lily Lake Art Studio opened to the public. Dave Stirling and Victor Palzer were exhibiting about a hundred canvasses of their work.

Mr. Stirling had spent the last ten years studying and painting the landscapes of the area, and Mr. Palzer was "one of the coming animal painters of the West and is showing many interesting studies of wild animal life."

In 1926, Guy Caldwell's Lily Lake Art Exhibit opened, and by 1930, the list of artists there was long and diverse. It included Grant Wood of Cedar Rapids, Iowa, Gustave Baumann of Sante Fe, New Mexico, Ilah Kibbey with her New England seascapes, Lyman Byxbe, the Omaha etcher (he returned for the summer in 1931 with Mrs. Byxbe and daughter Alice, and later became a permanent Estes Park resident), Dean Babcock, and many others.

Yes, Lily Lake "slept in silence"—until this week in our history, 1951.

Then, on May 25 of that year, "It is believed that a high wind piled waves against the earth dam at the northeast corner of the lake and eventually a break was worn. The low land between the lake and the South St. Vrain highway was quickly filled, allowing the water to run down the roadway. Finally, with pressure and erosion, the highway began breaking until, at about 5:30 a.m. there was a gap 50 feet across and 40 feet in depth. An immense volume of water then rushed down the Fish Creek bed carving deep gorges and carrying trees and boulders, emptying into Lake Estes."

The *Rocky Mountain News* stated on May 26, 1951, "Countless lives and several million dollars' worth of property were saved yesterday when newly constructed Olympus Dam on Lake Estes stopped a raging flood which developed from a broken dam at Lake Lily...

"Lake Estes, covering 163 acres, was designed primarily as an afterbay for the Estes power plant and a re-regulating reservoir of the Colorado–Big Thompson Project, but also was designed to absorb and control floods originating above Olympus Dam."

There was a lot of damage this week in 1951, but fortunately there were no deaths or injuries. Does what happened then seem to parallel the Lawn Lake flood of July 15, 1982?

Let's take a one-week step out of our week in history and go to June 4, 1951.

On that date "George Eiker, property owner along Fall River, appeared before the Chamber of Commerce board of directors. He pointed out that Lawn Lake holds back eight times the amount of water that Lily Lake impounded, and that the dike is no stronger than that of Lily Lake which gave way last week and did thousands of dollars' worth of damage to the South St. Vrain highway and to property along Fish Creek.

"'There is no Lake Estes above town to stop the waters of Lawn Lake,' he pointed out. 'A flood would devastate the National Park, then come down Fall River and take out homes and business buildings. There is even some question about what the flood would do to Olympus Dam'...

"He was named chairman of a committee composed of Ray Bradshaw and G.H. Gillan to meet immediately with proper authorities and alert them to the possible danger...

"They will ask that the irrigation company immediately put a guard on the dam so that a stoppage such as led to the breaking of the Lily Lake dike be averted. They will also ask that the National Park Service look into the feasibility of a 'protective dam' at the lower end of Horseshoe Park, above the Estes power plant."

But, there was no big rush—Lawn Lake also "slept in silence" for another thirty-one years.
[May 25, 1983]

JUNE

An Earlier 'Confluence Park'

The area north of Fall River and west of the Big Thompson, where those two rivers met, was proposed by the editor of *The Mountaineer* in 1908 as a good park site.

In 1922, Ted Jelsema and Frank Bond announced plans for construction on that site, which belonged to Bond.

By October, excavation was completed for a 40-foot by 80-foot swimming pool. When the pool was finished it had steam-heated water and a gravity filter purifier. The water depth ranged from one and a half to seven feet.

A 60-foot by 106-foot recreation hall was also completed. The following description appeared in the May 25, 1923 *Estes Park Trail:* "The main building houses the dance hall, soda fountain, bathing suit check room, etc. In the lobby just inside the main entrance is a large stone fireplace. In the west end of the lobby is an attractive rustic soda fountain. Here sandwiches will be served also. Steam tables and steam jets will keep the foods and hot drinks warm and will sterilize the dishes and glassware. Along the west wall of the dancing hall are located a number of rustic booths for dancers desiring fountain drinks, light lunches, etc. The floor will accommodate about two hundred couples. The orchestra stage is well built for carrying purposes and the slightest note is distinctly heard in the farthest corner of the room. The floor is exceptionally well built and properly prepared for the purpose. The swimming pool is one of the largest in the state and is heated by a large steam boiler. The pool is located between the dance hall and the Big Thompson River and is enclosed on three sides by change rooms, of which there are fifty, and also locker rooms. The ladies are also provided with a large dressing room. The pool is covered by large canvas roofing, and on the south end will be a nice sand beach on the bank of the river where bathers may sun and the children with their sand buckets may build their sand houses and enjoy themselves to their hearts' content.

"Another very attractive feature will be Forsythe's merry-go-round, one of the very best in the country. The Jelsema bowling alleys and the shooting gallery will also be located on the grounds of the amusement park.

"The boys plan to run a strictly clean and up-to-date place and will cater to the high-class trade that will be glad to come to them under those conditions."

And come they did—for over forty years.

This week in our history, on Memorial Day, 1923, the Riverside Amusement Park opened its doors "for its initial bow to the community and its visitors."

With music provided by various groups over the years, thousands danced and/or listened to the sounds of The Nebraskans, The Romancers, The Jay Hawks from Kansas University, Sarge Farrell, The Red Blackburn Orchestra, and Cocky Robbins and his 13-piece Dixieland orchestra.

Those groups got us through the 1920s and '30s, during which time Jelsema purchased Bond's interests in 1925, a new boiler was added to the swimming pool to raise the temperature to 84 degrees, and the interior of the dance hall was finished in a rustic style with 2,500 pine slabs from the Tie Camps down the North St. Vrain and in Big Elk Park. Swimming lessons were offered at the pool, the annual fireman's ball was initiated, and six cottages were built for employee housing. Cowboy dances became a weekly affair.

In 1933, "a new building to take care of the thirsty who will patronize his place" was built. The Dark Horse Bar was enlarged in 1937.

Oh yes, how did the Dark Horse get its name?

The *Estes Park Trail* asked that same question of Ted Jelsema in October 1969, and "he replied that before the repeal of prohibition he had purchased a merry-go-round in Greeley with the idea of installing it on the grounds.

"'When we tried to set it up, we found that some of the parts were missing,' he said, 'so we stacked the horses for a couple of years.'

"When the center obtained a 3.2 beer license Jelsema got the idea of using the horses for bar stools and booths."

In the forties there was a "coke side" and an adult side in order to cater to all visitors.

On January 4, 1946 Ted Jelsema sold the Riverside Amusement Park to Riverside Incorporated. Mr. and Mrs. Gale H. Gillan and Dean Sack of York, Nebraska were owners of the corporation.

The swimming pool closed in the forties, was covered with flooring, and became a roller-skating rink.

The fifties opened with Johnny Neill and his orchestra, and others included Sarge Ferrell, Gordon Dooley, Rolly Roberts, Ray Leach, Hugh Avis, and Jack Wheaton's Dixieland Band.

Dean Bushnell and his orchestra opened in 1952, and his "Sweet Swing with the Trumpet King" lasted for eight seasons.

Roller skating lost popularity, and the Darkhorse Theater occupied the stage over the former swimming pool from 1958 until 1969.

Music popularity was also changing, and for a few years bands like Lee Picket's Screamers and the Astronauts from Boulder brought new sounds to Riverside.

In 1965 the Riverside Dance Hall housed a family-style billiard and recreation center. The Super Cue can be chalked up as the end of an era.

The property was purchased by the Town of Estes Park in 1969, and after a farewell dance on January 31, 1970, the buildings were removed, and the 1908 "Park" became a park(ing lot).

[June 1, 1983]

Shootout in Muggins Gulch Spawns Mountain Jim Legend

Let's begin this week's column with a confession—what you are about to read is not entirely accurate.

We know that James Nugent, or Rocky Mountain Jim, was shot during the month of June 1874, in Estes Park, and died September 7, 1874, in Fort Collins.

So much for the facts—now on to the stories.

There is no known photograph of Mountain Jim, but after Isabella Bird first met him she described him as follows: "a broad, thickset man, about the middle height, with an old cap on his head, and wearing a grey hunting suit much the worse for wear (almost falling to pieces, in fact) a digger's scarf knotted round his waist, a knife in his belt, and 'a bosom friend', a revolver, sticking out of the breast pocket of his coat; his feet, which were very small, were bare, except for some dilapidated moccasins made of horse hide... His face was remarkable. He is a man of about forty five, and must have been strikingly handsome. He has large blue-grey eyes, deeply set, with well-marked eyebrows, a handsome aquiline nose, and a very handsome mouth. His face was smooth shaven except for a dense mustache and imperial. Tawny hair, in thin uncared-for curls, fell from under his hunter's cap and over his collar. One eye was entirely gone, and the loss made one side of the face repulsive, while the other might have been modeled in marble."

He had been practically scalped, his left arm broken, a finger bit off, and one side of his face, including an eye, had been mutilated in a fight with a bear.

She further wrote, "We entered into conversation, and as he spoke I forgot both his reputation and appearance, for his manner was that of a chivalrous gentleman, his accent refined, and his language easy and elegant."

When that English lady rode away, he said "You are not an American. I know from your voice that you are a country-woman of mine."

Jim made many claims regarding his identity. Some were: son of a British army officer, related to a Southern general, trapper with Hudson's Bay Company and American Fur Company, and one of Quantrell's Raiders. All, some, or none of these claims could be true.

Miss Bird also told of Griff Evans, from whom she was renting a cabin, and his feelings toward Jim: "He hates Evans with a bitter hatred, and Evans returns it, having undergone much provocation from Jim in his moods of lawlessness and violence."

It is a known fact that James Nugent was a perfect gentleman when sober, and quite the opposite when he was "in the cups," which was often.

Since we still don't know who he was, let's go on to what may, or may not, have happened this week in our history, 1874.

Abner Sprague, early Estes Park settler and local historian, was acquainted with both Griff Evans and Mountain Jim. In May 1922, he wrote an account of the shooting that took place during June of 1874.

"There have been several reasons given for the killing of Mountain Jim by Evans. Jim, in some of his drinking bouts with Evans, may have made threats against him, but I do not think Evans thought anything of it until after the shooting of Jim. Jim may have insulted some of the Evans family when drunk. He may have taken a stand against the land steal going on at that time in the Park, by which Evans was to profit; but none of these things had any bearing on the killing. Jim did not consider Evans a party to the quarrel that caused his death until after Evans had shot him down for his (Jim's) row with another man."

According to Sprague, "In June of 1874 an Englishman, claiming to be Lord Hague, came to the park to spend some time, and as the Evans home was the only place where visitors could be accommodated, he arranged to stop with them.

"He was given, and used the same sleeping quarters occupied by Miss Bird the fall before—a small one-room cabin near the main houses and road. Hague soon learned that Evans was flattered by being made a friend of by him and that things could be winked at, that could not be done in a civilized, or settled community."

A few days after Jim was shot Abner Sprague was near the Evans home and met a young man by the name of Brown, "who was the only witness to the shooting, outside of the interested parties."

Brown told him that Hague had decided that it would be a good idea to have company on his outing, and the company he desired was a "woman of the town" he had met in Denver. He didn't want to make the trip himself, so he had given Jim a hundred dollars for expenses and commission to bring her up.

He picked the right man, for Jim rushed off to Denver and paid his expenses. The trouble was that he didn't rush back with "the woman." A week or ten days later Jim returned broke and alone, and the next day while riding across the Park with Brown they met Hague and Evans at the foot of Little Prospect.

Hague wanted a report.

Jim may have made his report a little strong, for he said that the woman had told him "she would not go to the Park and spend the summer with the... English dog for all the money he had."

That did not set too well with Hague, and he called Jim a bloody thief, a liar, and a few other names. Jim responded by poking Hague off his horse with the muzzle of his cocked rifle, and "forced him to take back what he said."

The following day Jim and Brown were heading for Muggins Gulch and stopped for the horses to drink in Fish Creek.

Jim's horse only took a couple of swallows and started on. Jim was about in front of the Evans building when Brown "saw Hague and Evans come out of the little cabin occupied by Hague, Evans with a double barreled shotgun in his hands, and Hague urging Evans to shoot, as Jim was coming to kill him, and it was his duty to protect him. Evans threw up the gun and fired, missing both Jim and his horse; being urged to shoot again, he fired the other barrel and Jim fell from his horse."

Some references state that this shooting took place on June 10, 1874, which falls within this week of our history.

Since others say it happened on June 19, I have a good excuse to continue next week with different versions of how and why Mountain Jim was shot. [June 8, 1983]

Jim Dies Repeatedly; Story Keeps Changing

Last week we confessed that not everything about to be presented was accurate. That confession was followed by one version of how and why James Nugent (Mountain Jim) was shot in Estes Park during the month of June 1874.

This week we will prove the accuracy of our confession by relaying other versions.

In 1922, Ansel Watrous, pioneer newspaperman and historian, also published an account of the shooting. It is quite different from that published by Abner Sprague and reported last week.

According to Watrous, "...the most accepted theory is that 'Mountain Jim' became enamored of Evans' seventeen-year-old daughter and that the young lady's parents disapproved of his attentions to her. At any rate a coldness grew up between the two men, and 'Mountain Jim' in his cups had been heard to threaten to do Evans up. After the arrival of the young Englishman, whose name was Haigh, to take the management of Lord Dunraven's interests in the Park, the young lady became much attached to him. They were often seen riding together, which stirred 'Mountain Jim's' anger toward Evans to the very depths. On the 10th of June, 1874, only nine days before he received his death wound, he fired from ambush and tried to kill Evans, but fortunately his shot missed its mark. On the day of the fatal shooting, June 19th, 'Mountain Jim' appeared at Evans' cabin in a frightful mood, threatening to kill Evans and Haigh if they dared to come out in the open. At this Haigh, it is alleged, stepped to the door and fired the shot that a few weeks later ended the life of one of the most notorious characters that ever dwelt in the Rocky Mountains."

In his book *A Gallery of Dudes,* Marshall Sprague (no relation to Abner) tells of Lord Dunraven's activities in Estes Park: "He must find a real estate agent to start buying land soon. Evans and Mountain Jim now had Estes Park to themselves, but Dr. Hayden's surveyors were about to map the Longs Peak region, and homesteaders always flocked in after an area had been surveyed.

"The Earl's choice for his purchasing agent was the Englishman, Isabella Bird's 'Mr. Fodder' whose real name was Haig... You will recall that she introduced Jim to the dudish Mr. Haig, while comparing Jim's picturesque tatters to Haig's lemon-colored kid gloves and finding Jim ever so much more attractive...

"By the time of Dunraven's return West, Haig had bought Griff Evans' squatter's rights and his Fish Creek ranch buildings, retaining Griff as caretaker. But Mountain Jim had refused to sell, and had frightened the Englishman almost out of his lemon-colored gloves just by waving his gun."

The Earl of Dunraven wrote in his *Past Times and Pastimes,* again in 1922, that "Estes Park was inhabited by a little Welshman—Evans, who made a living I don't know how; and by Mountain Jim, who trapped—an extraordinary character, civil enough when sober, but when drunk, which was as often as he could manage, violent and abusive, and given to declamation in Greek and Latin. Evans lived in quite a decent, comfortable log-house, and Jim in a shanty some fifteen miles away [actually, more like four miles away]. Evans and Jim had a feud, as per usual about a woman—Evans' daughter. One fine day I was sitting by the fire, and Evans asleep on a sort of sofa, when some one rushed in shouting 'Get up; here's Mountain Jim in the corral, and he is looking very ugly.' Up jumped Evans, grabbed a shot gun, and went out. A sort of duel eventuated, which ended in Jim getting all shot up with slugs; no casualties on our side. He was not dead, but refused to be carried into Evans' house."

Harold Dunning, in his book *The Life of Rocky Mountain Jim*, wrote, "Jim was the lord and master of Muggins Gulch as it was known then. There arose the complex situation of getting Jim out of the way. None of the English dared to do it, for public sentiment would not have tolerated it, the public by this time being aware of, and highly indignant over Dunraven's land deal. Some time later Jim was riding his white mule passed Griff Evans cabin.

"Unseen by Jim, his old friend and neighbor appeared in the doorway with a shotgun at his shoulder. The gun roared, the charges struck an old stagecoach that stood in the road and rebounding, struck Jim in the base of the brain."

Dunning also interviewed Catherine Ellen (Nell) Evans Clemens, the fourth of seven Evans children. She "...hastened to tell me that her father was not a bad man just because he had shot James Nugent. She insisted that he was a very good and very kind man; but because this James Nugent had threatened to take away her sister, Jennie, who was only a girl in her teens, he killed him."

In *The Story of Estes Park* (c. 1905), Enos Mills relayed Abner Sprague's version of the story, then wrote, "This fellow, Brown, who was with Jim at the time of the shooting, and who gave Mr. Sprague the above account of it, disappeared a few days after the shooting and has never been heard of since. It is probable that Lord H. paid this important witness to disappear."

After all of this, what does Jim have to say about it? He wrote his version of the shooting to the *Fort Collins Standard,* and it was published in that paper on August 12, 1874: "...While riding peacefully along a highway in company with one William Brown, when near the residence of one Griffith Evans, he approached me with a double barreled shotgun in his hands, and when within a few steps, without warning, raised his gun and fired, killing the horse I was riding and inflicting a wound upon my person which fell me to the earth, and after I had fallen he deliberately walked up and shot me again through the head, turned upon his heel and disappeared in his house without even the inquirey whether I was dead." Jim went on to tell his side, basically placing the blame on the land troubles, and ending his story with "Great God! is this your boasted Colorado? That I, an American citizen who has tred upon Colorado's soil since 1854 must have my life attempted and deprived of liberty when the deep laid scheme to take my life has failed, and all for British Gold!"

Again quoting Enos Mills: "Meantime Evans visited Jim and asked to be forgiven; Jim's reply was said to have been: 'No, damn you, I'll forgive you with lead when I get well.' Jim did not get well and the talk of the time was that the attending physician was hired to put him out of the way."

James Nugent died on September 7, 1874.

The *Fort Collins Standard* on September 23, 1874, stated: "Evans was brought down from Estes Park on a warrant issued by the Coroner, last week, and had his trial before Justice Washburn, of the Big Thompson. He was discharged on the grounds of justifiable homicide. It is too bad that somebody couldn't be hung for not figuring up the cost to the county, before protecting their homes and firesides from insult and danger."

I guess my sentiments are with Jim, and I lean toward Brown's story to Abner Sprague, but even today no one knows exactly what happened.

So—you be the judge!

[June 15, 1983)

Stanley's Genius Evident Early

The month of June has a special significance for Estes Park.

It was on June 1, 1849, that Freelan Oscar Stanley and his twin brother, Francis Edgar, were born in Kingfield, Franklin County, Maine.

Toward the end of the month 54 years later, on June 29, 1903, F.O. came to the Park for the first time.

Then in 1909, on the 23rd of another June, F.O.'s Stanley Hotel opened with a convention of the Colorado State Pharmaceutical Association.

There is a lot being told of the hotel's 75-year history this year, so let's concentrate on the man and some of his many deeds.

A biographical sketch that appeared in the *New England* magazine of Boston in 1897 gave the following account of Freelan's schooling: "After receiving a common school education, he graduated from the Farmington Normal School and subsequently from Hebron Academy, and entered Bowdoin College, but left that institution after a year and a half, and began teaching."

A book put out by the University of Maine at Farmington, called *A Study in Educational Change—(1864-1874)*, by Richard P. Mallett, tells us that "Two of the most famous alumni of Farmington Normal were the Stanley twins... they entered the Normal School in

1869... Francis did not attend the school for the full two years, but his later accomplishments were to be recognized with an honorary diploma. Freelan O. not only graduated in the class of 1871, but went on to do considerable teaching."

A footnote expands: "For the first year after graduation he taught district schools in Andover, Farmington, and Lisbon. In the summer of 1872 he began to fit for college at Hebron Academy and entered Bowdoin in the fall of 1873 where he remained one year. Was Principal of the Mechanic Falls high School for several terms and then taught in Columbia, Penn.

"In 1880 he accepted a position in the Farmington Normal School where he remained one year, resigning on account of failing health to go into some less sedentary occupation."

While F.O. Stanley was going to school and teaching, a great change was taking place in photography.

He later wrote of that change: "In 1871, Dr. R.L. Maddox of London began experimenting with gelatin as a substitute for collodion, as a vehicle for holding the silver salts, and was sure to come into general use.

"For some time, the more ingenious photographers made their own dry plates. Fairly good formulas for making the emulsion, and directions for coating the plates, were published in the photographic magazines, but the work was too difficult, and too exacting for the ordinary workman, and most photographers continued to use the collodion wet plate.

"Of course an art as useful and as fascinating as the photographic art could not fail to attract the attention of men of intelligence, and business ability, so, in 1877, a man in St. Louis, J. Kenneth by name, conceived the idea of the mass production of photographic dry plates, and established a factory for that purpose.

"He did not make the complete plate, only the emulsion. This he dried, and pulverized, and packed it in opaque containers, and it was sold to photographers.

"They dissolved it in warm water, and each photographer made his own plates. This was too slow to suit the impatient American, and the industry did not prove to be a financial success.

"But a revolution in the photographic art had started, and the thrifty American could not let it rest. An opportunity was offered to establish a large, and profitable, industry, whose products would have a worldwide market.

"So by the end of 1881 there were operating in the United States three well-equipped dry plate factories—the Cramer and Seed factories in St. Louis, and the Eastman factory in Rochester.

"The change from the wet plate to the dry plate was so rapid, that in a very short time these factories were all doing a flourishing, and a profitable, business, and their combined capacity was sufficient to supply the demand."

In the meantime, his brother F.E. had become quite a crayon artist, but evolved into a photographer. He became interested in the new dry plate and began experimenting with it. By 1881 he had quit using wet plate entirely and was using his own dry plates.

F.O. continues, "It was then he began importuning me to join him in the manufacture of the commercial dry plates. But I had left the profession of school teaching, and was engaged in manufacturing at Mechanic Falls, Maine.

"I had purchased an abandoned factory, equipped it with machinery, and was engaged in the manufacture of supplies for schools. At that time mechanical drawing was rapidly being introduced into our schools, and on the market there were not suitable tools for that purpose that could be bought for reasonable prices.

"The great lack was a suitable drawing set the price of which would come within the reach of all pupils.

"I designed a drawing set containing a pair of compasses with a pen and pencil attachment, a rule, a triangle, and a protractor, all packed in a neat case that could be retained for one dollar. I took this to Boston, and showed it to Frost and Adams, and Mr. Lawrence, their purchasing agent, gave me an order so large that it nearly took my breath away.

"I went home and began the manufacture, on quite an extensive scale, of what we named 'The Stanley Practical Drawing Set.' It certainly seemed that opportunity had not only knocked at my door, but had flung the door wide open, and that I was certainly on the road to prosperity. But how little do we know what the future has in store for us.

"In less than a year, in a mysterious way, in the dead hours of night, the factory took fire, and the building, and its contents, were destroyed. The building was insured, but there was no insurance on its contents. And, as too frequently happens, I faced the loss of the savings of a lifetime."

He then took a job for one year as assistant cashier in a safe factory before joining his brother in the manufacture of photographic dry plates.

"We had, practically, no capital, no factory, and no customers. Cramer, Seed, and Eastman were amply able to supply the demand, and the dealers did not want to be bothered with any more dry plates."

What a way to start a business!

But the Stanleys remembered someone the others forgot: the consumer. "He, no matter who he was, where he was, or what he was, was always anxious to buy something just as good, cheaper, or to buy something better at the same old price. We decided to do both, to give him a cheaper plate, and a better plate. This was the problem that confronted us, and its solution meant success."

The twins developed a method of making plates faster, then they sold better plates directly to the photographers. They soon had orders from the largest dealer in the United States and had to increase their manufacturing capacity.

F.O. writes, "You may be interested to know that, up to this time we had hired no help. My brother assisted what he could, but I did most of the work.

"I was the general manager, the treasurer, bookkeeper and laborer. I never struck for increased wages, or shorter hours, although I worked an average of more than thirteen hours a day. I washed the glass, made the emulsion, coated the plates, packed them into the paper boxes, and the boxes into cases ready for shipment."

Their business continued to grow, and "One day I said to my brother that we ought to coat plates the same way paper is made. I had lived a number of years in Mechanic Falls, in which the leading industry was paper making, and I was thoroughly familiar with the paper making process.

"My brother agreed with me, and said he would design the apparatus for spreading the emulsion, if I would design the machine for carrying the plates along, and chilling them after being coated. We started at once designing and making this machine, and in less than 30 days we were coating all our plates on machine.

"And instead of a man and his helper coating 60 plates an hour, they were coating 60 plates a minute, and coating them better than they could be coated by hand."

The brothers kept designing equipment to improve their operation, and eventually moved to Massachusetts to save transportation costs.

They continued to outstrip their competitors with their revolutionary methods, and F.O. tells us, "Our sales continued to increase, and before 1900 our monthly sales had reached the one hundred thousand dollar mark. In the meantime we had become very much interested in the 'horseless carriage.' There was more fun in riding in a machine of our own make than there was in making dry plates, so in December, 1904, we sold the dry plate business to Eastman Kodak Co."

The Stanley Steamer automobile is also a story of its own.

So failing health took F.O. Stanley out of teaching in some "less sedentary occupation" in 1881. Twenty-two years later failing health brought him to Estes Park during this month in our history.

It seems that when his health began to fail, F.O. Stanley took new paths, found new interests, and did great things. As a patriarch of Estes Park, thanks to a fortune he made with dry plates during a previous "health failure," he:

- Improved the road from Lyons to Estes Park.
- Provided the first electric power plant in Estes Park.
- Initiated the first bank in Estes Park, and was its first president.
- Helped form, and was first president of, the Estes Park Protective and Improvement Association.
- Built the Stanley Hotel, which opened in 1909.
- Was instrumental in building water supply systems in Estes Park.
- Donated land for a sewer disposal plant.
- Brought visitors to Estes Park via Stanley Steamers from trains in Lyons, Loveland, Gold Hill, and Fort Collins.
- Many, many other things.

Freelan Oscar Stanley defied his doctor and lived to age 91, passing away in 1940.

[June 13, 1984]

An Elegant Hotel Opens Its Doors

Most people interested in Estes Park history know the stories of the Earl of Dunraven's desire and attempt to have the Estes Valley as his private hunting preserve. They know the stories of his methods to acquire the area, and of the homesteader's fight to keep it from him. They know of the sale of his six thousand acres to F.O. Stanley and B.D. Sanborn.

With that in mind, let us go to an editorial in *The Mountaineer,* Estes Park's first newspaper. On August 13, 1908 the editor wrote "If it was left to the people of the Park to name the new Hotel it would be called 'The Stanley.' The name Dunraven does not call up pleasant memories. About the only thing Dunraven suggests is a landgrabber who tried to convert the Park into a game preserve for his own use. Mr. Stanley's name will always be associated with the upbuilding of the Park, making it a place delightful for all the people. Give the splendid structure a fitting name."

A short article on August 27, 1908 states that "The name of the new hotel will not be 'The Dunraven,' but what it will be is not decided. Mr. Stanley is open to suggestions for a name, and offers a prize of ten dollars to the person suggesting the most appropriate and fitting name."

By petition of the people of Estes Park it was named "The Stanley Hotel"—a fitting name as requested by Mr. Stanley, a fitting name as suggested in the editorial.

Stanley had come to Estes Park in 1903 for his health. His doctor in Massachusetts had given him a few months to live—maybe a year if he went to a high, dry climate. He came to the high, dry climate of Estes Park every summer after that, became the Patriarch of Estes, and died in Estes Park in 1940 at the age of 91.

In 1909, Stanley arrived in Estes Park as usual, but this was to be a special year.

The *Rocky Mountain News* of June 23, 1909, printed: "Today is the most notable date in the history of the village of mountaineers for with the opening of the Stanley Hotel Estes Park takes first rank with any resort in the world."

The first convention at the Stanley was a group of Colorado druggists who convened during this week in our history. Since there were no color photographs then to let us see what the Stanley looked like when it opened, perhaps you will allow me to quote the *Denver Republican* of June 23, 1909, as it tells of the convention and the new hotel.

"Estes Park, Colo June 22—(Special)—The members of the Colorado State Pharmaceutical Association· were favored with a beautiful June day and the Big Thompson Canon was negotiated with perfect safety. At Loveland the members were met by a brass band and the full membership of the Loveland Retailers' Association, who with lusty acclaim dubbed the travelers the 'Colorado pill rollers.'

"Great excitement arose about half way up the canon, where the party encountered a big grizzly bear. Several of the party shot at it and upon cautiously approaching to give the 'coup the grace' with the bowie knife, found the bear filled with excelsior.

Each member of the party was presented with a dainty box luncheon by the Stanley Hotel management to stay the pill rollers until they could make the hotel.

"The caravan of 21 eight-passenger touring cars was met at the mouth of the canon by Mr. Stanley, who led the way to the magnificent new hostelry on Stanley Heights.

"The exterior of the hotel is of colonial design and its size can best be judged from the fact of its accommodating the entire membership of the convention, 150 strong, as well as its generous regular guest list.

"Its finest guest chambers surpass most of the presidential suites in this country and are finished in solid mahogany. Its cooking and heating is done entirely by electricity and smoke is an evil unknown.

"Views of Longs Peak, Tyndall and Andrews glaciers, the Twin Sisters and Black Canon ranges and the back range of the great continental divide are had from the parlors and banquet hall. The Big Thompson River, with its flower dotted meadows, shows magnificently from the hotel eminence toward the foothills.

"The parlors are handsomely carpeted with imported English fabrics woven especially for this house. The lobby, 100 by 40 feet, is furnished with special design, soft green leather chairs and settees and the walls are finished in soft crimson and white, with carpets to match.

"The banquet hall is done in dull mahogany and will seat 250 people. The main drawing and music room is one of Louis XVI design demask, bright frost and gold, and has a sweet toned grand piano. The smoking and billiard rooms are panelled in solid mahogany, with heavy beamed ceiling, and the smoking room has a monster fireplace of native lichen-covered gneiss. Large sun parlors open on the rear of the hotel and the front is serrated with a series of broad verandas.

"Two electric passenger elevators connect the three floors. The house has a telephone in every room and in every way is modern and complete.

"In connection with the hotel is a fine casino with a seating capacity of 600, which can be used for conventions, theater or social functions. It is furnished with a large upright piano and can accommodate a large orchestra.

"In the basement are two of the finest bowling alleys in this country.

"Every guest chamber is decorated with handsome pictures, faithful and pleasing, copies of the world's masterpieces, and every effort has been made by Mr. Stanley and his manager, A. Lamborn, to make the place attractive."

The following day *The Republican* printed: "Estes Park, Colo., June 23—(Special)—The pharmacists were lively today. They declared F.O. Stanley, the Boston millionaire and automobile inventer, and owner of the Stanley Hotel, a full fledged pharmacist. He accepted the honor gracefully, but admitted that all he knew of the business was that he had long been a drug on the market."

With all his personal achievements and the benefits those had on his fellow man, Mr. Stanley was far from a "drug on the market" even though he was unassuming as witnessed by his initial plan to call his hotel the "Dunraven."

We cannot end this any better than with a quote from *The Rocky Mountain Druggist*, a monthly journal of pharmacy, in July 1909: "With a site unequalled in Colorado, and this being conceded, on earth, nature has combined with the great heart of a philanthropist to perfect a dwelling place for man that gods may envy."
[June 22, 1983]

Long's Sighting of Highest Peak

Between 1803 and 1819, the United States, through negotiations with France, Great Britain, and Spain, had extended territorial limits west to the Pacific Ocean and south into Florida.

Considered by many the father of American exploration, Thomas Jefferson sent several expeditions into those unexplored areas, two of which were the Lewis and Clark journey and that of Zebulon Pike.

There were many reasons for these expeditions. Reliable maps and scientific data of plant and animal life were some, but not the least of the reasons were strategic, political, economic, and military; in short, to strengthen our claims to territorial rights in North America against British, Canadian, and Spanish competitors.

The War of 1812 caused exploration activities to be suspended, and it was several years before expeditions of consequence were again sent out.

In March of 1817 James Monroe became the fifth president of the United States. He had previously been Secretary of War, so he had an interest in the military. With his appointment of John C. Calhoun as Secretary of War, Monroe's time in the White House was a time of opportunity for the army, and consequently for renewed explorations.

Let's back up a little to December 30, 1784, when Stephen Harrison Long was born to Moses and Lucy Long in Hopkinton, New Hampshire. He was their second child, and the first of thirteen children to survive.

There was not much money, but he managed to receive enough preliminary education to be admitted to Dartmouth College in 1905 at the age of 21, where he studied medicine, surveying, and navigation.

In December 1814, the War Department issued a commission as a second lieutenant to Stephen Long. It was sent to the wrong city and Long did not receive it for three months, but then promptly accepted it. He was an assistant professor of mathematics at West Point for a year, then managed a promotion to Brevet Major and a transfer to the topographical engineers.

Long was involved in several exploratory missions over the next few years, and in 1818 he submitted a proposal for steamship exploration into the West. Secretary Calhoun had an obsession with impressing the Indians, and immediately accepted the proposal. He authorized Long to supervise building the boat, and to recruit scientists so the expedition "would enlarge general knowledge about the West, as well as gather military and geographic information."

Long's original design was for a smaller crew than eventually started, and he revised plans and had other delays. He was extremely busy while the "Western Engineer" was being built, but found time to court and marry, on March 3, 1819, Martha Hodgkins of Philadelphia.

On May 5, the expedition finally headed out with Secretary Calhoun's order to explore the region between the Mississippi River and the Rocky Mountains.

By September the explorers had reached the area of Omaha and decided to stay there for the winter. They had cabins built by October, and before heading back to Washington to discuss plans with Calhoun, Long named the camp "Engineer Cantonment."

The many mechanical and other problems of the "Western Engineer," its average progress of six to eight miles a day, the Panic of 1819, sickness and injury, and unrealistic original expectations caused rumors of waste, incompetence, and corruption. Those rumors preceded Long and were taken seriously by Congress. The War Department budget was severely cut.

The scientists were allowed to continue in 1820, but without the "Western Engineer." Their budget would buy horses so they could follow the Platte River to its source, move south to the source of the Arkansas, where half of the party was instructed to continue east along the Arkansas, while the rest were to go south and west to find the source of the Red River.

Long went from Washington to St. Louis with the promise that funds would be there for him. He waited in vain for $2,000 that came weeks after he left without supplies. He arrived at Council Bluffs on May 27.

Political and fiscal pressures forced Calhoun to cut his budget and show more results. That forced Long's party to travel rapidly, with few supplies, little equipment, and no time for thorough study.

The expedition consisted of Stephen Long, commander; John Bell, journalist; Edwin James, botanist, geologist, and surgeon; Titian Peale, assistant naturalist; Thomas Say, zoologist and ethnologist; Samuel Seymour, landscape artist; William Swift, assistant topographer and commander of escort; seven civilians and seven soldiers.

The three weeks of waiting for funds caused them to travel across their assigned route in hotter, drier weather than they would have had earlier.

They reached the Sand Hills on June 19, having been short of food for some time. Along the South Platte there was much discontent about the "intense reflections of light and heat from the surface of many tracts of naked sand."

Long named the area east of the Rocky Mountains the "Great American Desert," and is credited with delaying settlement there for 50 years.

But what does all of this have to do with this week in the history of the Estes Park area?

On June 27 the party entered what is now Colorado near present Julesburg, and of another day in this week of our history, June 30, 1820, Dr. James wrote: We soon remarked a particular part of the range, divided into three conic summits, each apparently of nearly equal altitude. This we concluded to be the point designated by Pike as the highest point."

Their conclusions were wrong, for what Pike had called highest peak, or "Grand Peak," is now called Pikes Peak, and what Long's party saw that day and called "Highest Peak" is now called Longs Peak.

On July 14 Edwin James and four others climbed Pikes Peak. Major Long noted on July 15, 1820: "...Dr. James having accomplished this difficult and laborious task, I have thought proper to call the peak after his name... Pike had indeed given us notice that there is such a peak, but he only saw it at a distance." On Long's map it is called James Peak.

There is no recorded ascent of Longs Peak until 1868, on another day, during another week in our history. [June 29, 1983]

JULY

Estes Family's 'Pioneer Day' Reunion

The anniversary of the birth of this great country of ours has been celebrated more than 120 times since Joel Estes looked down from Park Hill in 1859 and viewed the "park" that was to bear his name.

According to a letter written by W.H. McCreery in 1925, a Fourth of July celebration was held in Estes Park in 1876, about a month before Colorado became the "Centennial State."

Although that was possibly the first one, let us jump ahead 51 years to 1927, when Estes Park had what may have been the most significant Fourth of July celebration in its history.

Dr. Homer E. James was chairman of the committee in charge of arrangements for the 1927 celebration, and much of what he and his committee arranged has been a part of Estes Park ever since.

It was labelled "Estes Park Pioneer Day," and one of the events was a parade in which pioneers of Estes Park participated and/or were represented.

"The parade started at 10 o'clock and was an elaborate showing of pioneer and historical portrayals and of beautiful floats, decorated cars, riders, orchestras and other parade features.

"The parade led to the grounds east of town where the granite marker and bronze tablet on the old Estes homestead was unveiled and where a program of music and speeches was given."

Another quote from the July 8, 1927 *Estes Park Trail* states that "Estes Park's first Wild West show, the Stampede of July 3 and 4, was a drawing card for thousands of the Park visitors the past weekend."

Since "Western Week" in Estes Park is coming up in a couple of weeks, perhaps you will allow me to save the "Stampede" and some other rodeo related items until then.

For this week, though, we mentioned the destination of the parade, so let us get on with the granite marker and bronze tablet, which reads:

**In memory of Joel Estes,
Discoverer 1859 Oct. 15 1866
Pioneers Patsy Estes
Sarah Estes Mollie Estes
Milton Estes Joel Estes
F.M. Estes J.W. Estes
Presented by the
Chamber of Commerce and
The Grand Children
Milton Estes Joel S. Estes
Edwin Estes
Mrs. C.H. Graham
Mrs. W.I. Myler
Mrs. C.D. Taylor
Noma Ritters**

Descendants of those first pioneers also had their first family reunion in Estes Park that Fourth of July.

Family members who attended were: Hon. Joel Stollings Estes, former Justice of the Supreme Court of Oklahoma, grandson of the pioneer, Joel Estes; Harry Ruffner, grandson, and Mrs. Ruffner, of Denver; Eugene Ruffner, son of Harry, and his wife and son of Port Arthur, Texas.

Also, Mrs. Mary Stiles, granddaughter, Sidney, Iowa; Mrs. Emily Graham, granddaughter, Thurman, Iowa; Edwin Joel Estes, grandson, with his wife and family from Longmont; Mrs. Charles H. Babcock, great-granddaughter, and Mr. Babcock, Los Angeles, California; Earl W. Roberts, great-grandson, with Mrs. Roberts and family of Beverly, Nebraska; C.M. Hiatt, second cousin, Mrs. Hiatt and family of Colorado Springs; Harold Estes, great-grandson, Sydney, Iowa.

Also, Mrs. Anna Estes Seeger, second cousin, Tabor, Iowa, her sons Ernest H. and Francis M. of Smol, Nebraska, and grandson Leonard John Stewart of Lexington, Nebraska; Myrtle Palmer Ellis, great-granddaughter of Joel Estes, Riverton, Wyoming; Milton Estes, grandson, Sydney, Iowa; and Mrs. Philina Palmer, granddaughter, and the oldest relative in attendance at the celebration, from Riverton, Wyoming.

Two of the speakers at the unveiling were Judge J.E. Estes from Oklahoma and Harry Ruffner of Denver.

This list is quite a contrast to the 150 or so Estes Family members who converged on Estes Park for their second reunion in August 1981.

Another is planned for the first week of August 1983.

So the pioneer celebration and the stampede went off in great style when an estimated 40,000 people, larger than any previous crowd ever in the Park at one time, came to help celebrate.

I would like to share parts of an editorial regarding that Fourth of July, 1927: "Heretofore Estes Park has always considered itself too busy in selfishly grabbing dollars on that day to really be patriotic and to provide some entertainment and attention for its multitude of visitors.

"Now Estes Park knows it pays to be patriotic and that it pays to provide attractions for its visitors that does not require a coin in the slot to have the privilege of enjoyment.

"Estes Park has also learned what a fine thing cooperation, that is genuine and not pretended, really is. Every person who took part is entitled to generous credit for the remarkable success of the celebration, and with the exception of Dr. H.E. James, no individual or organization is entitled to special mention or credit above any other.

"For weeks previous to the event, Dr. James devoted his whole time to working out the celebration. He was compelled to neglect his own business and his only remuneration is the gratitude of the visitors and the knowledge Estes Park's first patriotic celebration was a really BIG success.

"...we can expect even better things as we gain ideas and experience."

The parade has become an institution; the stampede, or rodeo, has become an institution; the granite marker and bronze tablet are prominently permanent; and the Estes Family is finding its way back more often lately.

In a couple of weeks let's see what else started then and is still with us.
[July 6, 1983]

Retracing Our Indian Heritage

About noon on Tuesday, July 14, 1914, a train pulled into Longmont.

Tom Crispin emerged confidently carrying his suitcase.

Sherman Sage, dressed in his blue cloth chief-of-police uniform, with its slightly baggy knees, stepped down with a roll of blankets under his arm.

Gun Griswold, looking somewhat embarrassed, was fanning himself with some eagle feathers, his share of the luggage.

From Longmont they were taken by automobile to Longs Peak Inn, arriving late in the afternoon. There Enos Mills helped them make plans for a camping trip.

Surely thousands—no, millions—have come to these mountains to go camping, so what made this particular trip worth mentioning, and who were those guys, anyway?

Griswold was a 73-year-old Arapaho Indian, who had been a judge among the Arapahos under United States law.

According to Oliver W. Toll, in 1914, Griswold was retired "on a moderate allowance, taken out in rations, I believe. No one could help respecting him.

"He spoke little, had a great deal of dignity, and was treated with consideration by the others. They said that his only son had been killed a few months ago by another Indian, which accounted for Griswold's lack of spirits."

Sage was 10 years younger than Griswold, possibly 10 times as energetic, and "as jolly as Griswold was quiet." Sage was Chief of Police on the Wind River Reservation in Wyoming, where he, Griswold, and Crispin lived.

Toll wrote of him, "...a good man for his position, responsible, brave and cool. He impressed one as particularly trustworthy and honest. Added to this, he was a pretty shrewd old Indian, and a good judge of people."

Sage had been wounded in the right hand at the battle of Clear Creek.

Tom Crispin was about 38 years old. He was the official interpreter for the Arapahos on the reservation, had a daughter ready to enter college, and a son, Tom Jr., who he called Buster.

Tom (Indian name, White Horse) told Toll that the U.S. Government had arbitrarily assigned names among the Indians, and he was to give their new names to the Arapahos.

Toll said, "They took it all as a huge joke, as we would if we were to be assigned Indian names... Tom was named Crispin because he was christened on St. Crispin's Day, although he assigns as an additional reason that an aunt of his married an Englishman by the name of Crispin."

Now we know a little of who they were and where they came from, so we can get on with why they came.

A two-week pack trip had been arranged by Harriet Vaille, Edna Hendrie, and Oliver Toll (Colorado

Mountain Club), and outfitted by Shep Husted, a local guide with extensive knowledge of the area.

The purpose of the trip was to learn the Arapaho names of the trails, peaks, and other landmarks in the Estes Park–Grand Lake area.

Shep could provide the names currently used, and Griswold and Sage, who had lived in the area years earlier, could provide the Arapaho names through interpretation by Crispin.

The white man gave names to things as they affected pioneer life, and the Arapaho names reflected their life.

The white man named many things after people, while the Arapaho named many things after events that had taken place.

We'll just touch on a few things in this column, but if you want to try the Arapaho language or get a more detailed account of the trip, the Estes Park Public Library has the small book *Arapaho Names and Trails* by Oliver W. Toll.

One place to start is the entire Estes Park basin. It was called "The Circle" by the Arapaho. "Two Guides" was the name for Longs Peak and Mt. Meeker, a landmark visible for miles.

Once, when the Arapahos were on the south side of the summit of Taylor Peak, they killed a man from an invading tribe. That man's hair was cut straight across his forehead, and since bangs were usually worn only by girls, the unusual event prompted what we know as Taylor Peak to be called "The Bangs."

"The Big Trail" was certainly descriptive of the Estes Park–Grand Lake Trail. That was their name for Flattop Mountain.

The "Child's Trail" was so steep that children had to get off and walk on the way up. We know it as the Ute Trail up over Trail Ridge.

There was a trail called "Dog Trail" because Indians often used dogs to carry loads over it, especially in winter when a load could be easily dragged. That trail went up Fall River and was another way to Grand Lake.

Bierstadt Lake was the Arapaho's "Hanging Lake." That seems appropriate when viewed from above.

Another example of naming things after events is "The Shirt" (Prospect Mountain). On the northern slope of that mountain four or five hostile Indians were killed. One of them was wearing a shirt.

North of Estes Park is a ridge that has been called for many years the "Needles." The Arapaho name of "Lumpy Ridge" seems to have returned.

Lily Lake was called "Beaver Lodge" and Lily Mountain was "Beaver Lodge Mountain."

The Arapahos told several stories of battles with other Indians—Shoshones and Utes near Devil's Gulch, Utes in several other places, Apache in Beaver Park.

The Apache war party of about 50 men had come in from the southwest and been met by the Arapahos in Beaver Park a little south of the High Drive.

They eventually made a stand for over a day near the Hondius Ranch, where they built a fort of rocks.

Sage's older brother was wounded in that fight, but as he (Sage) was only four years old at the time, he did not remember all the details of the battle. If Sage was 63 in 1914, that battle would have taken place in 1855.

We could go on and on, but these highlights will at least let you know of one more thing that happened during this week of our history.

The route of that naming trip took the party to the Hondius Ranch on July 16. They scouted around on July 17, left on the 18th, went up Windy Gulch and camped at timberline below Trail Ridge.

The 19th saw them up Trail Ridge and to the west, camping at Poudre Lakes.

On July 20 they went to the crater of Specimen Mountain, over Milner Pass to spend the night at Squeaky Bob Wheeler's place.

They proceeded over Lulu Pass to the head of the Michigan on the 21st, up Sawtooth Mountain and back to Bob's for the night of the 22nd, and on to Grand Lake the 23rd.

Around there on the 24th, up the North Inlet Trail on the 25th, over Flattop, part way up Hallet Peak, and in to Mill Creek Ranger Station on the 26th, then back to Estes Park on the 27th, where they were all housed in a hay barn on Shep's ranch.

Toll wrote, "Wednesday, the 29th, the party broke up. The Indians went by stage to Fort Collins, where at the Agricultural College they made two dictaphone records, and then took the train for Cheyenne."
[July 13, 1983]

Western 'Stampede' Launched Rodeo Tradition

Two weeks ago, we touched on Estes Park's Fourth of July celebration of 1927, but really didn't get into the rodeo, or stampede, that was a big part of the festivities.

We also mentioned the parade, but perhaps you would like a few more details.

The primary idea in the selection of parade winners was their relation to and portrayal of pioneer or historical subjects.

"Mrs. M.E. March's first prize winning float was most clever. A tiny log cabin representing her early homestead was the subject portrayed, and Mrs. March herself, dressed in pioneer fashion, drove her horse, Hallie, which she had when she came to the Park 15 years ago."

Mrs. Minnie E. March was awarded a $150 oil painting for the grand prize.

There had been other parades and rodeos before 1927, but after we mention a couple we will come back to that important year.

There was a parade on the Fourth of July, 1914.

The July 11 *Estes Park Trail* stated "The celebration started at 10 a.m. with a grand parade led by several children who sang 'America' with all the spirit of patriotism in their young souls. They were followed by horseback riders, carriages and automobiles, all gaily decorated with flags, and red, white, and blue ribbons.

"The procession marched from the village to the Elkhorn Lodge, from there to the Stanley Hotel, and then back to the village."

As far as a rodeo, or facsimile thereof, in 1914, we quote: "...As the race started, her horse swerved and broke the track, throwing Miss Rockwell to the ground. She was immediately surrounded by sympathetic friends who were ready and anxious to offer aid. But the gritty young lady thanked them, declining aid, as she was not hurt.

"A gentleman then tried to ride the horse, but was obliged to put a curbed bit on him before he could control him. Mr. Jasper Edmonds and Mr. Charles Thomas rode the bucking horses and Dean Edmonds won first and Ted Wight second in the boys' horserace."

In 1924: "The Aviation Field will be the scene of the Estes Park Rodeo events to be staged July 4 and 5." There was also a 10 a.m. parade.

July 10, 1925: "A rodeo will be held each Sunday at the Stanley Aviation field in which a group of wild horses and cattle will participate."

June 10, 1927: "Estes Park expects more than 20,000 additional visitors on this day. The afternoon of the Fourth, a big wild west show will be staged at the new amusement grounds being built by the Stanley Corporation a half mile east of the village.

"Race track, grand stand, polo grounds and aviation field and hanger are being built to accommodate the crowd. The wild west show, which will be an annual affair, will be in charge of Jack Elliott of Cheyenne Frontier fame, and Lester (Scotty) Scott.

It is planned to make this event one that in a few years will rival the famous Pendleton Roundup and the Cheyenne Frontier Days celebration.

"...The track, corrals, grandstand, etc., will be of the very best and latest design for such a wild west show, and everything is planned to make both the show and the accommodations for the spectators the very best possible...

"There will be two corrals at the east end, inside the enclosed field for the animals used in the riding contest; one will be the large corral for the horses and wild Brahma steers and will be equipped with a side delivery chute into the field; the other will be a smaller corral for the animals used in bulldogging and calf roping.

"At the west end of the enclosed field there will be another catch corral in which all the animals may easily be driven as soon as another event or another rider is ready...

"The best of strong pole plank construction will be used in the corrals and the track will likewise be enclosed both on the inside and outside with ample fencing.

"The grandstand will accommodate about 1,500 spectators and from the west end of the grandstand on around the west end of the track there will be parking space for automobiles."

The events of that 1927 Stampede are as follows:
1. Boys' calf riding—$5 first, $2 second; each day.

July

2. One quarter mile cow race—Purse $120. Each day, $30 first, $20 second, $10 third. Race subject to approval of the starter.
3. Calf Roping Contest—Purse $200. (Two calf average, one to be caught each day) $5 entry fee to be added. $100 first, $60 second, $40 third.
4. Pony Express Race, ½ mile—Purse $100; $50 each day. $25 first, $25 second, $10 third. $5 entry fee to be added and split. Pair of boots on last day given by Cook's Log Cabin Cafe.
5. Bareback Bucking Horses—$5 per mount. Eight horses to be bucked each day.
6. Buckboard Race—Each day; $25 first, $15 second. Jack Elliot Stetson hat given by Frontier Committee.
7. Feature Event—Purse $120. Brahma Steer Riding. Each day; $30 first, $20 second, $10 third. Stampede Trophy Chaps given by Elliott and Scott best time in two days.
8. 300 Yard Cow Horse Race—Each day; $25 first, $15 second.
9. Bulldogging contest—Purse $150. Each day; $50 first, $25 second.
10. Deadwood Stage Coach Race—$25 first, $15 second.
11. Trick and Fancy Riding and Roping.
12. Wild Cow Milking—Each day. $15 first, $10 second.
13. Potato Race—July 3rd. Wyoming vs. Colorado. $20 to the winning state.

14. Musical Chair—July 4th. $20 to the winner.
15. Colorado Championship Bucking Contest—Purse $220. Day money, $50 and silver mounted saddle from Denver Post first, $30 second, $20 third. $5 entry fee each day added to the purse.
16. Free-for-all Half-Mile Race—Purse $160. $100 to be given by Stanley Hotels. Each day; $40 first, $30 second, $10 third. $10 entry fee each day added to the purse.
17. Wild Horse Race—Each day; $20 first, $15 second.

On the third of July the attendance was about 10,000 with near 12,000 on the Fourth. A total of $5,000 in prize money went to the contestants on the two days.

Part of a July 8, 1927 editorial reads, "...Scott and Elliott may feel proud of the fact their first attempt was so successful and so well received. As experience is obtained with the region and type of clean entertainment required, this first annual Wild West Show will improve and attract greater and greater patronage."

Since these columns are intended to tell of something that happened during the week in which they are published, some year in our past, let's legalize this one.

On July 18, 1941, a headline in the *Trail* stated "Rooftop Roundup Will Attract Thousands." I had not seen the Estes Park Rodeo referred to as "Rooftop" before 1941.

Two weeks ago we did not mention the rodeo grounds in Stanley Park. This week we did, and if you will allow

one more quote from July 1, 1927: "As manager of the grounds Mr. Scott is ready to give any necessary and helpful information concerning any phase of the Stampede and... will be there on the grounds to welcome all."
[July 20, 1983]

Toll Road Offered Estes Park – Lyons Link

Alexander Q. MacGregor came west from Milwaukee in 1869.

The young lawyer soon became clerk of the Arapahoe County Court at Denver, took the Bar examination, and was admitted to practice law in Colorado Territory.

In 1872, he came to Estes Park on a camping trip. The following year he went back to Wisconsin, married Clara Heeney and returned to Estes Park.

On his trip to the Park in 1872, A.Q. MacGregor traveled over a road that was described by Isabella Bird in 1873 as follows: "Evans takes a lumber wagon with four horses over the mountains, and a Colorado engineer would have no difficulty in making a wagon road.

"In several of the gulches over which the track hangs there are the remains of wagons which have come to grief in the attempt to emulate Evans' feat, which without evidence, I should have supposed to be impossible.

"It is an awful road... When Evans, who is a very successful hunter, came here, he came on foot, and for some time after settling here he carried the flour and necessaries required by his family on his back over the mountains."

Abner Sprague wrote of the road to Estes Park, "Before the time of barbed wire these fences had to be made of posts and poles.

"Large pitch pine posts were used, and a mortise and tennon fence built, three or four poles making a panel. For this material roads were made well back in the lower mountains.

"One of these roads was made and used for timber as far on the Estes trail as Little Elk Park, coming into it from the south.

"Joel Estes used this trail and continued up the branch of the Little Thompson, now known as the Muggins Gulch. This trail he improved to a road for a cart, after settling in the Park, and could be negotiated by a four wheel rig by careful driving and lots of motive power.

Griff Evans and Mountain Jim improved the Estes road in the late 1860s to that described earlier by Isabella Bird.

That "improvement" was not good enough for A.Q. MacGregor.

What he traversed in 1872 would never do for the permanent settlers and tourists that he envisioned coming to this beauty he had fallen in love with, this Park called Estes.

His granddaughter, Muriel MacGregor, wrote in 1935: "...by grant of the Territorial Legislature, Alexander MacGregor was given exclusive right to build and maintain a road between Glen Evens, a few miles this side of the present Lyons, and Estes Park, and collect a toll thereon for 10 years to recompense him for the cost of building the road. The toll road system was used extensively in early Colorado history to open up the mountain region.

"My grandmother invested $10,000 of her own wealth in the undertaking. An entry in the diary of my grandfather for March 13, 1875 tells that my grandparents incorporated the project on that date as the 'Estes Park Wagon Road Company.'

"The road was commenced in '74 and for the first part of the work no diary record has yet been found among my grandparents' effects.... There was no town at the present site of Lyons, but the huge red sandstone formation was named Steamboat rock, then as now, and around its base came the roadway.

"For three miles the road followed the North St. Vrain, but then turned to the right through a narrow, rocky defile and climbed upward for three miles.

"From the mountain top thus attained, the Little Thompson was to be seen on the north, flowing through deep canyons, and southward, the sparkling waters of the St. Vrain, as well as the multi-colored hogbacks in the east.

"As the road continued westward along the mountain tops, it reached high summits and then dropped into deep ravines. A pretty valley, Musk Park, was passed through and then the road climbed to a particularly high point from which the plains and the far away Platte River came into view.

"The road then descended to the valley of the Little Thompson near the present site of the Mining ranch house. From that point, the present North St. Vrain highway practically follows the course of the toll road.

"...Week by week the diary records progress as the road camp moved steadily westward, the site too often recorded by landmarks now forgotten. At last, we find the important entry in the diary for Wednesday, July 28, 1875: 'Opened road and commenced taking toll at noon.'

"The toll gate was located near the present site of the Mining ranch house, Alonzo Parsons being the first toll gate keeper. The account book for the toll road receipts does not seem to be in existence, but the diary gives the information that the toll collected for the first three and one-half days, that is, until the end of July, was $31.95.

"The usual charge appears to have been a dollar a team each way, but rates were given those who used the road regularly of 50 and 60 cents."

MacGregor had many problems with the road. Heavy rains washed out portions of the road and bridges, fences were pulled down, and finally a cloudburst caused so much damage that he sold out at a loss to a group from Longmont.

Abner Sprague wrote of MacGregor's road in 1922, "The Park end of this road terminated at the MacGregor Ranch, crossing the Big Thompson on what is now the Crocker Ranch, and going direct from there to the ranch in Black Canyon.

"Mr. MacGregor operated this road for about 10 years, then sold it to Longmont parties. Before the time the charter was to expire by time limit, 1895, 20 years, the owners decided it was too good a thing to lose, and would grow better as time went on. So they cut a few corners, made some slight changes, and secured a new charter to run for another 20 years.

"They raised the toll charges and refused to reduce it for the poor lumber, wood or pole hauler who traveled it regularly, but charged him the same toll as the man who used it only once.

"The settlers along this road and those who had to use it to get to and from the valley, came to the conclusion that 20 years was long enough to pay toll on the same road, particularly since the law gave the people the road after that length of time. These teamsters refused to pay toll, hitched onto the gate and pulled it down the road."

After some court action, the toll that began during this week in our history, 1875, was permanently removed, and Estes Park had a free road to Longmont and Denver.

That road was poorly kept up until the coming of F.O. Stanley and his Steamers, but that's another story.

[July 27, 1983]

AUGUST

Famous Friendship Founded in EP

Deacon John Adams, husband of Susanna Boylston, was a constable, militia officer, farmer, shoemaker, and a deacon of the North Precinct meetinghouse in Braintree, Colony of Massachusetts Bay.

Their son, John, was born in 1735, graduated from Harvard in 1755, married Abigail Smith in 1764, denounced the Stamp Act in 1765, joined his cousin Samuel Adams and the Sons of Liberty in 1766, was sent to the first Congress in Philadelphia in 1774, nominated Washington as Commanding General at the second Congress in 1775, and was a pillar of the Revolution as he rallied support throughout Europe. He won recognition of the U.S. by the Hague in 1782, was first American minister to England after the war, and became the second President of the United States in 1796. John Adams died July 4, 1826, the same day as Thomas Jefferson.

On July 11, 1767, John Quincy was born to John and Abigail Adams. He travelled to Europe with his father during the Revolution, was educated in Paris, Leyden, and Harvard where he graduated in 1787. He married Louisa Catherine Johnson ten years later. John Q. helped draft the peace treaty for the War of 1812, was Secretary of State under James Monroe, helped formulate the Monroe Doctrine, and was elected the sixth U.S. President in 1824 by the House after no candidate won an electoral college majority, was defeated by Andrew Jackson in 1828, and later served 17 years in Congress, where he died in the Speaker's Room on February 23, 1848.

Charles Francis Adams was born to John Quincy and Louisa in 1807, graduated from Harvard in 1825, married Abigail Brooks in 1829, was elected to Congress in 1858, and in 1861, was appointed minister to Great Britain by President Lincoln. He was a candidate for President in 1872, but Greeley was nominated. C.F. Adams died November 21, 1886.

On February 16, 1838, Henry Brooks Adams was born, the fourth child of Charles Francis and Abigail. He was named for his first American ancestor, who left England in 1638.

Henry wrote in his autobiography, *The Education of Henry Adams*, regarding his schooling: "He hated it because he was here with a crowd of other boys and compelled to learn by memory a quantity of things that did not amuse him. His memory was slow, and the effort painful. For him to conceive that his memory could compete for school prizes with machines of two or three times its power, was to prove himself wanting not only in memory, but flagrantly in mind. He thought his mind a good enough machine, if it were given time to act, but it acted wrong if hurried. Schoolmasters never gave time.

"In any and all its forms, the boy detested school, and the prejudice became deeper with years. He always reckoned his school days, from ten to sixteen years old, as time thrown away.

"...the happiest hours of the boy's education were passed in summer lying on a musty heap of

Congressional Documents in the old farmhouse at Quincy, reading *Quentin Durward, Ivanhoe,* and *The Talisman,* and raiding the garden at intervals for peaches and pears. On the whole he learned most then."

Of his later education, Henry Adams wrote "For the purposes of future advancement, as afterwards appeared, these first six years of a possible education were wasted in doing imperfectly what might have been done perfectly in one, and in any case would have had small value. The next regular step was Harvard College. He was more than glad to go. For generation after generation, Adamses and Brookses and Boystons and Gorhams had gone to Harvard College, and although none of them, as far as known, had ever done any good there, or thought himself the better for it, custom, social ties, convenience, and above all, economy, kept each generation in the track. Any other education would have required a serious effort, but no one took Harvard College seriously. All went there because their friends went there, and the College was their ideal of social self-respect.

"Harvard College was probably less hurtful than any other university then in existence. It taught little, and that little ill, but it left the mind open, free from bias, ignorant of facts, but docile. The graduate had few strong prejudices. He knew little, but his mind remained supple, ready to receive knowledge."

Henry began to write in college and later travelled to Europe—Germany, Italy, France, and with his father to England where he was a secret correspondent who sent articles back regarding affairs of state.

He received knowledge in many ways, and in 1870

Henry Adams became an assistant professor of Mediaeval History at Harvard.

In June 1872, Henry and Marion ("Clover") Hooper were married.

Professor Adams continued to learn and to teach and to write. After seven years his new course on the history of the United States from 1789 to 1840 spawned his nine-volume *History of the United States During the Administration of Jefferson and Madison*, among other works.

After the death of his wife, a trip to Japan, and the death of his father, he finished the ninth volume of his history in 1888.

Henry Adams died in 1918.

All of this may or may not be of interest, but what do five generations of one of America's most prominent families have to do with Estes Park during this week in our history?

Clarence King, who was a Yale graduate, prepared specifications for a survey of the western U.S. from California to Nebraska in a 100-mile-wide strip along the 40th parallel to include railroad advancement in the West.

The twenty-five-year-old King sought and received an appointment from Secretary of War Stanton to proceed and "to examine and describe the geological structure, geographical condition and natural resources" in that region, and he was to accomplish it in two seasons.

After he began in 1867, it was five years before the field work was complete to the Continental Divide, and another eight years before the results were compiled.

In 1879, President Hayes appointed Clarence King

the first director of the United States Geographical Survey. He took office in March 1880, but resigned later that year due to conflict of interest with his personal holdings.

King died of tuberculosis in Atlanta in 1901.

Henry Adams had few friends, but one of his childhood friends, Frank Emmons, had become a geologist and joined the 40th Parallel Survey. Adams, in his continual search for knowledge, had written an article on geologists, and in 1871 he went west to find Emmons and to learn more of the land of the future. He did not find Emmons, but latched on to another party of the group at Laramie.

They went south from there and "One morning when the party was camped high above Estes Park, on the flank of Longs Peak, he borrowed a rod, and rode down over a rough trail into Estes Park, for some trout."

Adams fished all day and the time got away from him. Darkness fell, and he tried unsuccessfully to find his trail, but turned back. His *Education* continued: "There was but one cabin in the Park, near its entrance, and he felt no great confidence in finding it, but he thought his mule cleverer than himself, and the dim lines of mountain crest against the stars fenced his range of error.

"The patient mule plodded on without other road than the gentle slope of the ground, and some two hours must have passed before a light showed in the distance. As the mule came up to the cabin door, two or three men came out to see the stranger.

"One of these men was Clarence King on his way up to the camp."

Adams and King became immediate and life-long friends. One coming from the west, the other from the east, they met at Griff Evans' cabin on August 5, 1871. The next day they went to the camp and stayed awhile before parting, but those two men, prominent in separate fields, each contributed to the other's continued education for the next thirty years.
[August 3, 1983]

Misguided Souls in 'Elkanah Valley' Received Inspiration (and Damnation) from Rev. Lamb

"My first view of Estes Park and the Longs Peak range, was on August 10, 1871. A sight sublime to the eye, and almost solemn, to a mind contemplative of God's wonderful works."

So wrote Rev. Elkanah J. Lamb in his *Miscellaneous Meditations*.

Who was this man whose mind contemplated God's works?

He arrived in this world at South Bend, Indiana, on January 1, 1832, the third of nine children born to Esau and Elizabeth (Moon) Lamb.

In 1842, the family moved to Iowa, where settlement was new and Indians plentiful. Rev. Lamb wrote in *Past Memories and Future Thoughts*, "Many times old Chief Black Hawk and his successor, Keokuk, came to our cabin, Black Hawk's eyes were keen and piercing, like an eagle's; Keokuk's, of mild demeanor. The Indians dubbed him 'Squaw,' because he was for peace, Black Hawk was for war.

"But living here in the wilds, away from all relatives and civilized life, was not agreeable to my mother."

They sold out and moved back to Indiana in 1844. As Elkanah matured he met "a young lady of sterling worth, friendship's golden chain bound us together, and soon ripened into intense affection... indulging in love's sweet dream," but "a tragic episode (not necessary to mention) severed these relations for all time."

With a friend he left home, and practicing the cooper's trade, they made barrels and split rails across Indiana, Illinois, Missouri, and into Iowa.

There he met another young lady, and again "friendship ripened into mutual affection." They "concluded to quit the delusive scenes of single blessedness, entering upon marital relations."

After farming in Iowa for a while they left on May 5, 1857, and moved to Linn County, Kansas, where, according to Enos Mills, Sr., they arrived with other Free Staters on June 6. (Enos Mills, Sr., had married Ann Lamb, a relative of Elkanah's, in 1855.)

The next few years brought a prospecting trip to Colorado, conflicts with border ruffians, the Civil War, and a literal contribution to the term "Bleeding Kansas" when, on October 25, 1864, Elkanah was wounded in the shoulder during the Mine Creek battle between those of differing opinions,

The Lambs moved again to Nebraska. "Then came the turning point in life, involving denial, eros-bearing, and trials. With my earliest recollections, in reference to right living, always came the thought, in fact, the conviction, that I must preach the gospel."

He became a preacher and "we traveled far and wide over Nebraska, organizing churches and Sabbath-schools."

Their two daughters, Minnie and Ida, died, and less than a year later Elkanah's wife, Jane, also "went out from our home to be buried with the little lambs that had gone before."

After examination by four theologians, Elkanah Lamb was ordained in the United Brethren Church on April 17, 1870.

The Bishop asked for missionary volunteers for California and Colorado. The new Rev. Lamb gave his name for Colorado.

In the meantime, on September 29, 1868, he married again, and the widow Jane Morger accompanied him through life.

Rev. Lamb preached his first sermon in Colorado at Ralston in May 1871. He established and laid the stone foundation of the first United Brethren church in Colorado, "Eleven miles from Denver, seven miles from Brighton, close by the Denver and Cheyenne railroad, not far from the Platte River." It was dedicated on the first Sunday in August.

This circuit-riding preacher covered many miles and preached to many groups, and during this week in our history, "The ninth day of August we started on a long contemplated trip to the mountains and Estes Park, going by way of Ralston and Ni Wot, and holding services as we went at those places."

During his first stay in the Park, Lamb climbed Longs Peak alone and a few days later acted as a guide for others.

He was directed to travel through Nebraska for the church, but in September of 1873, he and his family returned to Colorado.

The Lambs, "with some outside help," made a road to their claim near Longs Peak and built a home which they eventually expanded.

Rev. Lamb's "territory or travel extending from the South Platte canyon north to the Big Thompson and the Cache La Poudre rivers" caused him to be gone for weeks at a time. When home he was a guide up Longs Peak.

Eventually the Lambs had neighbors: the Edwin Gillette family; Mrs. Josie Babcock and her son Dean; Mr. Bitner, who built a large lodge and dining hall, which he named the Columbines; the John Moreland family; Mrs. Mary Kirkwood and her sons, Stephen and Charles Hewes.

At a gathering of neighbors Charles Hewes offered a resolution which was seconded, "That our valley be formally named and christened, Elkanah Valley, after [Lamb's] first name, Elkanah, meaning 'Whom God Possessed.'"

Lamb's Longs Peak House was purchased by Enos Mills in 1902 and became Longs Peak Inn.

The list could fill a large volume with happenings from the life of Elkanah Lamb, but perhaps a couple of remarks from the memoirs of Eleanor E. Hondius will help us picture him on a Sunday morning:

"Finally, the Rev. Elkanah Lamb became our regular minister; in fact, he appointed himself, saying 'As long as there are eight or ten people gathered together in the name of the Lord, I will preach.'"

"He was of the United Brethren sect, and certainly a great believer in hellfire and damnation; his sermons were never less than an hour in length.

"He was at least six feet five inches tall, and he wore a long black frock on Sunday. On the table which served as a pulpit he would lay a snowy white handkerchief. As he preached, his voice would get louder and louder, and finally he was shouting. Suddenly, he would stop, pick up the handkerchief, and give his nose a violent blow. (I always thought this trumpeting would put Gabriel to shame.) Then Mr. Lamb would start the sermon again, and go back up the scale."

Mrs. Hondius' opinion of Rev. Lamb may have been slightly influenced one Sunday when young Eleanor of the Elkhorn Lodge "had a lot of dishes to wash, and about three-quarters of a mile to walk to get to church. When I arrived, the services had started and the congregation was praying.

"I opened the door and crept in, hoping that I had not been noticed, only to hear the Rev. Lamb say, 'Dear Lord, forgive these lazy, good-for-nothing people who cannot get up early enough on Sunday morning to get to church on time.'"

Enos Mills wrote, Elkanah Lamb "is honest, sincere, and poor; poor because always generous—Though rarely agreeing with him on any proposition, yet for years I have probably been his most intimate friend—He is a lover of nature—He is passionately fond of music—although he gives excessively he does not pose as a saint—One cannot accompany him far without being ennobled. Back of his lines and his life is a noble man."

Rev. Lamb died in 1915 at the age of eighty-three and was followed two years later by his wife. They are buried in Ft. Collins, Colorado.

[August 10, 1983]

'New' Trail Improved Access to Longs Peak via Chasm Lake

The trail up Longs Peak was improved in 1921, and the *Estes Park Trail* (newspaper, not dirt and rock) published several stories about it on August 19th of that year.

A front-page story says that "Supt. Way has a new survey run and trail built on it that when completed will give an easy grade all the way to boulder field on Longs Peak and which opens up an entirely new territory to tourists.

"The old trail mostly followed the ravines and in many places had a grade of 30 to 40 percent. Because of its location it suffered terribly from the large amount of water from the watersheds above, while the new trail is laid out with an easy 15 per cent grade all the way and follows the ridges most of the way and reaching the moraine east of the peak, which opens up entirely new territory, and thence over the Chasm Lake ridge. The new trail is scientifically built to suffer the minimum damage from rains and melting snows and is so located that there is seldom much of a watershed above it.

"While the new trail is just a trifle longer than the old one, the easier grade enables the tourists to make quicker time and with much less fatigue, and there is no doubt but that the peak, which is said to be the most scenic in the United States, will become more popular than ever with the tourists."

Another story states that "Ranger McDaniel gave the new trail up Longs Peak a try-out Monday by making the ascent unaided on a motor-cycle nearly to timberline."

Also that "Mac Dings, The Columbines Guide, has had wonderful success with his Longs Peak parties this season. Every party that he has started has reached the top, with the exception of one. In that case the wind was so very high that the party could not safely reach the summit. Mac has a faculty of making every one of his Peak trips a pleasure trip."

The next week's *Trail* told us that "Guide Mac Dings reports that he saves three-quarters of an hour on each trip up Longs Peak now that the new trail is in use. Ranger 'Tex' Eddins and his crew have done a nice piece of work on the Peak; but we must also give credit to Dean Babcock, who laid out the trail and has general supervision over it."

But what I really wanted to mention is that during this week in our history, on August 16, 1876, "Rev. W.H. McCreery made the ascent of Longs Peak, and guided a party, including four persons beside himself, although much of the way was without a trail. He was able to do this from a description of the route given verbally by Abner E. Sprague, who had then made several trips."

That August 19, 1921, *Trail* goes on to announce that "This summer the 'Lure' of the Peak, of which there is such a magnificent view from his cottage, has been making a pretty strong pull on Mr. McCreery, and a few days ago he confided to some friends his desire to at least attempt to climb the 'Keyhole' on the 45th anniversary of his former climb.

"...Rev. L.C. Struble and his wife, Mrs. (J.D.) Hyde

August 163

and Mrs. Chas. Berger, formerly Miss McCreery, and son Russel, gave countenance and character to the expedition by conducting it to Longs Peak Inn. The other five members of the party took horses at the Inn, and tackled the climb with the following result: Mr. McCreery 82 accomplished his object, the Keyhole; Kenneth Hyde, 18, also stopped at the Keyhole, and kindly accompanied and assisted the older man on his way back over Boulder field, while Chas. Berger, 52, Earl Hyde, 20, and Miss Mary Struble, 14, made their way successfully and expeditiously to the top, and all made the return trip in good time. Notwithstanding the fierce wind on boulder field and at the Keyhole and a slight pelting with sleet, the trip was enjoyed by every member of the party.

"Mr. McCreery has been a resident of Loveland and vicinity from 1874 to 1919 with Estes as his summer home for practically all that period.

"He first visited the Park in 1874 and filed on the McCreery Ranch in 1875. He is among the last survivors of the older generation of Park settlers. His present home is with his daughter, Mrs. Tuggy at 1042 W. 7th Street, Riverside, Calif. He will leave the Park toward the close of the month for California."

Rev. W.H. McCreery was born in Westmoreland County, Pennsylvania, on November 17, 1839, was graduated from Westminster College in 1870, ordained a minister in the United Presbyterian Church in 1874, came to Loveland, Colorado, and organized the United Presbyterian Church in 1875 with initial membership of 15.

In the fall of 1882 he was appointed superintendent of schools in Larimer County, and was in general a contributor to the benefit of those living in Estes Park and the county.

On June 16, 1926, Rev. McCreery, still strong of mind and body, died at the age of 86 in a fire aboard a sleeping car of the Union Pacific on his annual return to Estes Park.

[August 17, 1983]

Climbing Longs Peak in 1868

"August 20. The party destined for the ascent of Longs Peak, consisting of Major J.W. Powell, W.H. Powell, L.W. Keplinger, Sam'l Garman, Ned E. Farrell, John C. Sumner, and the writer, left camp at the west side of Grand Lake, each mounted, and with one pack mule for the party."

So wrote William N. Byers, editor of the *Daily Rocky Mountain News* of Denver.

We are fortunate that Mr. Byers was not only a pioneer newsman, but that he liked to climb mountains as well. We are doubly fortunate that he was able to attach himself to the various explorers and government surveyors who found their way to the Estes Park area.

The September 1, 1868, edition of the *News* gave Byers' day by day account of the first documented ascent of Longs Peak by John Wesley Powell and party.

After the group left Grand Lake they tried to approach over Pagoda but couldn't make it. They left their horses to graze "on the short young grass of the mountain side," and by the 22nd of August they camped at Timberline in Wild Basin. Then "Some explorations were made, however, preparatory to tomorrow's labor; the most important by Mr. Keplinger, who ascended to within about eight hundred feet of the summit, and did not return until after dark."

Keplinger had almost made a solo climb to the top.

He wrote in 1919, "I went ahead, into and through the Notch—at the northerly edge of the Notch, Estes Park was before me for the first time—All was well until I paused and looked down." He turned back to camp and arrived about an hour after dark on a stormy night.

Then, on that big day in our history, 1868, William Byers wrote: "August 23. Unexpectedly the day dawned fair, and at six o'clock we were facing the mountain. Approaching from the south our course was over a great rockslide and then up a steep gorge down which the broken stone had come. In many places it required the assistance of hands as well as feet to get along, and the ascent at best was very laborious.

"There was no extraordinary obstacle until within seven or eight hundred feet of the summit. Above that point the mountain presents the appearance, in every direction, of being a great block of granite, perfectly smooth and unbroken.

"Close examination, however, removed this delusion in some degree, and we were most agreeably surprised to find a passable way, though it required great caution, coolness and infinite labor to make headway,–Before ten o'clock the entire party stood upon the extreme summit without accident or mishap of any kind."

L.W. Keplinger was the first of the party to stand upon the summit.

While on top, "Barometric and thermometric observations were taken to determine altitude, and a monument erected to commemorate our visit. A record of the event with notes of the instrumental readings was deposited, along with other mementos, in a tin case in the monument, and from a flag-staff on its summit a flag was unfurled and left floating in the breeze."

After a three-hour stay on top and a two-hour descent with a short snow squall, observation of "wagon loads" of grasshoppers and how "upon these the bears were feasting," they camped for the night on "the most westerly branch of the St. Vrain."

The next day Byers wrote: "August 24—We had been gone only five days; had been eminently successful, and of course were satisfied; the more so because the mountain had always before been pronounced inaccessible, and ours was the first party that had ever set foot upon its summit."

Who was it who had pronounced the mountain inaccessible in the past? Perhaps Mr. Byers thought his readers had a short memory, or perhaps he forgot that after his attempted ascent on August 20, just four years earlier, he wrote in the September 23, 1864 edition of the *News* that "We had been almost all around the Peak; so far that we could see all sides of it. We are quite sure that no living creature, unless it had wings to fly, was ever upon its summit, and we believe we run no risk in predicting that no man ever will be, though it is barely possible that the ascent can be made."

Remember that we said earlier that the Powell party made the first documented ascent of Longs Peak?

The following statement was taken from *The Western Mountaineer*, Golden City, Jefferson Territory, September 6, 1860: "Gold Hill, Aug. 28, 1860. Mr. Cromer, of this place visited Long's Peak, last week, and scaled the summit, the view from which he describes as grand in the extreme. Four days were required for the journey thither and back; and no traces were discovered of any person having previously visited the summit since the Government party, many years ago."

Did Mr. Cromer climb Longs? Or was it maybe Meeker? And who was the government party? Major Long never went near Longs Peak, nor did Fremont. When the Byers party climbed Meeker in 1864, "as far as man can go," they added their names "to the five registered before." Perhaps Cromer was one of them.

Also, remember the Arapaho Indians who came in 1914? One of them was Gun Griswold, and his father was Old Man Gun. Griswold told of an eagle trap Old Gun had on top of Longs Peak. It was a hole to climb into with a stuffed coyote for bait, and from which he could grab an eagle when it came down. Griswold claimed to have climbed up with others to see the trap 55 years earlier, which would be 1859. They had climbed up from the south and the trap "was then pretty well filled in."

Indians probably had climbed Longs before the white men knew it was there, but when the Powell party went up they saw no signs that others had gone before.

Perhaps they hadn't. Possibly they had.
[August 24, 1983]

SEPTEMBER

Parting Vision of Rocky Mountain Jim

"His chivalry to women is so well known, that Evans said I could be safe and better cared for with no one. He added 'His heart is good and kind, as kind a heart as ever beat. He's a great enemy of his own, but he's been living pretty quietly for the last four years'... and as he commended me to Mr. Nugent's care, the two men shook hands kindly."

So wrote Isabella Bird in December, 1873, of her last day in Estes Park. Griff Evans had escorted her as far as James (Mountain Jim) Nugent's cabin down Muggins Gulch, and Jim was to accompany her to Namaqua and St. Louis (in the present Loveland, Colorado, area) where she would board the stage to Greeley on her long journey back to England.

During that first leg of the trip more of Jim's true character came through as they had their last long ride and their last long talks.

"'Jim' shortened the way by repeating a great deal of poetry, and by earnest, reasonable conversation, so that I was quite surprised when it grew dark. He told me that he never lay down to sleep without prayer—prayer chiefly that God would give him a happy death."

They stayed the night at the house of a man named Miller, who "came out and said his house was 'now fixed for ladies.'"

They reached Namaqua the next sunset and went on

the three miles to "the queer little place where they 'keep strangers' at St. Louis."

The landlady was very excited when she found out that the "quiet, kind gentleman" was Mountain Jim. She confessed that she used to frighten her children when they were naughty by telling them that Jim "came down from the mountains every week, and took back a child with him to eat."

Miss Bird then wrote, "The children got on his knee, and, to my great relief, he kept them good and quiet, and let them play with his curls."

Later, when all was quiet and Isabella was writing a letter to her sister, "Mr. Nugent copied for himself the poems *In the Glen* and the latter half of *The River Without a Bridge,* which he recited with deep feeling... He repeated to me several poems of great merit which he had composed, and told me much more about his life."

She took one last opportunity to urge Jim to reform his ways, especially his drinking.

"Ay, too late. He shed tears quietly. 'It might have been once,' he said. Ay might have been. He has excellent sense for everyone but himself, and, as I have seen him with a single exception, a gentleness, propriety, and considerateness of manner surprising in any man, but especially so in a man associating only with the rough men of the West. As I looked at him, I felt a pity such as I never felt before for a human being."

The next morning, Isabella Bird left on the Greeley stage and watched Mountain Jim "with his golden hair yellow in the sunshine, slowly leading the beautiful mare over the snowy Plains back to Estes Park."

Yes, Jim went back to Estes Park, and the following

June was shot and mortally wounded by the same Griff Evans who spoke so warmly of him in the first paragraph of this week's column.

We spent two weeks this past June relaying several versions of how and why the shooting took place. Now we must report that during this week in our history, on September 7, 1874, James Nugent, or Rocky Mountain Jim, died at the Collins House in Fort Collins, Colorado.

From the post-mortem examination we learn that "there was a fracture of the skull at a point corresponding with the wound at the back of the head, in which was imbedded a battered piece of lead." After more probing into the brain cavity, "was found a much larger piece of lead" which "undoubtedly was the nucleus of the fatal inflammation."

A Coroner's jury "found that James Nugent came to his death from gunshot wounds at the hands of Griffith J. Evans."

Evans was discharged on the grounds of justifiable homicide.

But, what about Isabella Bird?

She returned to her life in England.

Her biographer, Anna M. Stoddard, tells us that "Her guide in the Rocky Mountains, known as 'Mountain Jim,' was a Mr. Nugent, a man of good birth and university education, who had unhappily yielded to ruinous habits and had drifted down to the precarious freedom of a trapper's life by 1873, when she met him."

During the weeks they knew each other, Jim's help and consideration eased the trials of Isabella's experience, and her concern and influence raised Jim temporarily from the depths of his "ruinous habits."

"When she had to bid him farewell at Namaqua, Mr. Nugent broke down completely. 'I shall see you again,' he reiterated. 'I must see you again' ...Then they promised each other that after death, if it were permitted, the one would appear to the other.

"On July 25, came the distressing news that he was dead."

Yes, the erroneous message that reached Miss Bird was that Jim had been killed rather than wounded.

She left for Switzerland the next day, "occupied with the remembrance of their mutual promise." Later at Interlaken, as she lay in bed one morning, Isabella "saw 'Mountain Jim' in his trapper's dress just as she had seen him last, standing in the middle of her room. He bowed low to her and vanished... When exact news of his death arrived, its date coincided with that of the vision."

This week in our history—September 7, 1874.
[September 7, 1983.]

Improvement Association Left Fishy Legacy

"ESTES PARK, COLORADO
SEPTEMBER 22, 1906

"We the undersigned, residents or owners or agents of property, in Estes Park, Larimer County, Colorado, being desirous of Associating ourselves for Social purposes, and for furthering the beautifying of said Park, and not for pecuniary profit, do hereby associate ourselves together, under the following Statements and Stipulations.

"First, the name of our Society shall be The Estes Park Protective and Improvement Association.

"Second, the particular business and object for which our said Association is formed, shall be to promote Social intercourse among ourselves, and to suggest, provide for, and maintain improvements, such as roads, trails, fish hatcheries, tree planting, forestry, and any like attempts intended to be of use and benefit to the members of this Association and its associates."

The rest of the fifteen "Statements and Stipulations" give the general rules of order, duties of officers and board members, and rules and regulations of membership. F.O. Stanley was the first president, with C.H. Bond as secretary.

As noted, one of the main objects of the Protective

and Improvement Association was to build a fish hatchery for the purpose of keeping the local streams stocked. To have the tourists report on excellent fishing in the area would be just the advertising needed to bring more visitors, consequently more dollars, to Estes Park.

From a 1912 report by G.H. Thompson, the first hatchery superintendent, we learn that "Money was raised and a hatchery was built, and opened on the 22nd day of July, 1907."

From Pieter Hondius, treasurer, it is revealed that "The cost of building and equipping the hatchery was $3,352 of which $712 was donated in labor and $2,640 in cash."

The Protective and Improvement Association had a ladies auxiliary, and they did an excellent job of raising money. *The Mountaineer,* on August 27, 1908, reports: "The third of the Fish Hatchery dances was held at the Estes Park Hotel Tuesday night, and the usual good time was reported by all who attended. The program consisted of eight dances and two extras, and the music was of the best. The large dancing floor was crowded.

"People were carried to the hotel by the auto companies for fifty cents for the round trip, and the receipts donated to the hatchery. The amount realized from the evening has not been made known, but it is understood to be above the $100 mark."

(The same ladies auxiliary group in 1912 formed their own society known as the Woman's Club, and later started the Estes Park Public Library.)

In 1909, P.J. Pauly donated two small fish ponds, F.O. Stanley donated the upper big pond, and Bruce Eaton the lower big pond. That same year the superintendent's cottage was built at a cost of $1,944.

By 1912 the hatchery had been leased to the State of Colorado.

So, the fish are being well taken care of. What else did the Protective and Improvement Association do?

It was made up of environmentalists, who worked to protect trees, flowers, and other plants, "and has been instrumental in the arrest and conviction of three individuals, two for killing deer and one for killing beaver."

Members watched over cabins and cottages when their owners left, "and when in the winter of 1911 some of the cottages were broken into and property stolen, two of the theives (sic) were put in a safe place for a year."

They built and improved trails and roads. They advertised Estes Park in many ways. "The Association has also assisted Mr. Enos A. Mills in his travels and agitation for the creation of the Estes Park National Park."

Mr. Thompson also tells us that "from the time the fish has deposited her eggs in the gravel, to the time that they must pass through the hatching stage and then the absorption stage, only three percent of fish survive, leaving 97 percent loss, while in the hatchery we save 75 percent."

The hatchery was doing a good job of getting 75 percent of the eggs to hatch, but a story in the May 20, 1921 *Trail* states, "It is a well-known fact among our fishermen that many thousands of the fish taken from the hatchery are devoured by the larger fish when they are planted in the streams."

The following week the *Trail* reported: "At a well

September 177

attended and enthusiastic meeting held in the Odd Fellows Hall Wednesday evening an organization to be known as the Estes Park Fish and Game Association was formed. The purpose of this organization is the construction of maturing ponds and protection of game.

"The association has the assurance of the entire output of the Estes Park fish hatchery."

With the limited research I have done, I don't know when the Estes Park Protective and Improvement Association ceased to exist, but C.H. Bond was its president in 1915, when Rocky Mountain National Park was dedicated. From 1918 to 1923, he was in the state legislature.

Could the Fish and Game Association have been a continuation of, or replacement for, the Protective and Improvement Association?

On January 30, 1970, almost 64 years after the Protective and Improvement Association began, another organization known as Beaver Point Association was incorporated. The officers were Giles Gere, president; Lisle Ware, vice-president; Herman Duerksen, treasurer; Mrs. Blanche Gere, secretary. Their purpose was to "become involved in planning and uses of Beaver Point area in and around Estes Park."

That association began with two studies—one to explore the advantages and disadvantages of annexation, and the other about the creation of a sanitation district in the Beaver Point area.

At their July 9th meeting in 1971, the Beaver Point Association was changed, or expanded, into the Estes Valley Improvement Association.

Giles Gere was re-elected president; E.R. Anderson,

first vice-president; W.O. Myers, second vice-president; Harper Glezen, treasurer; Mrs. Leonard Murphy, recording secretary; and Mrs. Gere, corresponding secretary.

"The Estes Valley Improvement Association, formerly the Beaver Point Association, is a non-profit, voluntary organization of individuals, business establishments, and agencies having in common a concern for the improvement of all areas in and around Estes Park, Colorado, through cooperative and constructive action. This organization will endorse those individuals, corporate or governmental developments in the community which seek to enhance the character of the community, and to oppose those influences or trends which, in the judgement of its members, encourage blight and deterioration."

Like those of the Protective and Improvement Association before them, the goals of the EVIA are honorable ones, and their accomplishments should be long-lasting.

The Protective and Improvement Association began during this week in our history, 1906. Their goal of a fish hatchery was accomplished in 1907, and it was certainly long-lasting. It was another September in 1981 when the *Trail-Gazette* reported that the State of Colorado would permanently close the Estes Park fish hatchery in early 1983.

The Lawn Lake Flood of July 15, 1982, destroyed most of the breeding ponds, and the hatchery was indeed closed on schedule.

But during the 75 years it existed, thousands of people, with thousands of poles, pulled out thousands

of trout—made possible by the Estes Park Protective and Improvement Association.
[September 21, 1983.]

Estes Park Given Its Name

Thousands of events have occurred between September 19 and September 25 in the Estes Park area. One that is of historical significance to all of us is the naming of Estes Park.

Back in the old days, or even today, a mountain enclosed meadow was, or is, referred to as a "park."

In 1859, while on a hunting trip with one of his sons, Joel Estes popped over the hill and saw this beautiful mountain-enclosed meadow, with the Big Thompson meandering through like a silver ribbon carelessly dropped on a carpet. That was October 15, not exactly this week's history, and no, he didn't name it.

He did, however, move his family to this mountain-enclosed meadow the next year. They settled over where Fish Creek meets the Big Thompson, about where the part of Lake Estes on the south side of Highway 36 is now.

A few years later, in August of 1864, William N. Byers, editor of the *Daily Rocky Mountain News,* came to this area with a group of men for the purpose of climbing Longs Peak. That did not happen during this week in our history either, but Mr. Byers went back to Denver and wrote about his six-day trip and attempted ascent.

On September 22, 1864, William Byers wrote of his arrival to this mountain-enclosed meadow, "Reaching the head of the creek, and surmounting a low grassy divide, Estes Park lay before us, a very gem of beauty."

Such is the way this park, in which the only occupants were a family named Estes, got its name in print for the first time.

[September 22, 1982. This article was the first "This Week in Estes Park History" column that appeared in the *Estes Park Trail-Gazette.]*

Seasonal Rites Endure

"The day was warm, no wind, and no clouds visible anywhere most of the day, and Longs Peak and Mount Meeker reared their snowy crests far into the marvelously blue sky, with a pretty variegated foreground of evergreens and colored aspens of every autumn hue on the Twins and the nearer mountains."

No, the above quote did not come from a Chamber of Commerce brochure intended to entice flatlanders up for Aspenfest. In fact, it's not that uncommon a description of the Estes Park area in September or early October.

What makes it worthy of attention today is that it was first written during this week in our history, 1925. The occasion was to report on the first annual community and fete day held at the Estes Park Golf and Country Club grounds.

The Chamber of Commerce was involved, as their program committee prepared "a varied and appealing series of events with prizes offered for winners in all events."

That sounds familiar too, doesn't it? But the events weren't quite the same as those of an Aspenfest of the 1980s. They hadn't considered a Scottish Festival with bagpipes, caber toss, and stone throw. No one even thought of using the natural resources for an elk dung marble shoot. And it only lasted one day, rather than three weeks.

September

But that one day was a big one! "Almost every person in the Park was on hand to enjoy the occasion and at lunch time picnic parties were to be observed thickly seated all about the grounds near the club house."

Before lunch though, "at ten o'clock the golf fiends—men and women, started two nine-hole events that were won by Joe Mills in 35 strokes. His handicap allowed him 39 strokes in which he sunk his ball on the tenth green. Mrs. Joe Mills sunk her ball on the tenth in 75 and won the ladies' event."

The other events took place after lunch, and the results are as follows:

"Andy Archer won the men's long distance golf drive, and Mrs. A.K. Holmes won the long distance drive for ladies.

"There were three entrants in the old settlers' race which was won by Dr. James with Carl Piltz second, who says that foot racing does not agree with corns.

"Girls' running race, 10 years and under, Martha Finn, first; Madge Hall, second.

"Girls' running race, over 10, Dorothy McDonald, first; Mildred Perkins, second.

"Boys' running race, 10 and under, Theodore Holmes, first; Walter Schwilke, second.

"Boys over 10, John McGraw, first; Paul West, second.

"Ladies' indoor baseball throw, Wilma Baldridge, first; Mrs. Lee Tallant, second.

"Men's indoor baseball throw, Newell Anderson, first; Paul West, second.

"Babies hobby horse race, Jack Stith, first; Glen West, second.

"Obstacle race, Paul West, first; Norton Billings, second.

"The ladies' ball game was won by the girls team by a score of 11 to 10, three innings.

"The men's ball game went four innings and was won by the high school boys over the town team with a score of 10 to 3.

"Prizes were given winners of firsts and seconds in all events, except the golf games and the golf drives, in which firsts only were awarded."

The year 1926 brought the second annual community picnic and fete day, which "is for every resident of the Park, every visitor in the Park, and every friend of the Park in the valley who can get here."

A tradition had started, and it continued every year through 1931. After that, I did not find the "picnic and fete day" mentioned, perhaps because of the Depression.

We had mentioned some of the differences in the events, compared to Aspenfest. There were a few other differences as well.

Why do we have Aspenfest?

Certainly it is because of the beautiful time of the year. It also provides fun, enjoyment, festivity, and a holiday atmosphere. What does all that bring? People to Estes Park—people who will not only enjoy themselves, but will also frequent the businesses of the area and add to the local economy.

Nothing wrong with that, but let's compare with the picnic and fete days of yore:

1926: "All of the stores and the bank will close from 11 o'clock until five o'clock. This day will be a real community holiday and there will be no excuse for staying away."

1925: "The village itself presented a thoroughly deserted appearance. Practically all of the business houses were closed and a visitor who arrived in the town about 1 o'clock was unable for some time to find someone to tell him the reason for the deserted appearance of the streets. He stated that for a few moments the whole thing seemed uncanny—and then he discovered that everyone was at the country club enjoying the time of the season. There he found everybody happy and participating in the various events with a hearty good-will that was pleasing to behold."

Enjoy the time of the season.

[September 28, 1983]

Estes Park's First Press Agent

"I wish I could let those three notes of admiration go to you instead of a letter. They mean everything that is rapturous and delightful—grandeur, cheerfulness, health, enjoyment, novelty, freedom, etc. etc. I have just dropped into the very place I have been seeking, but in everything it exceeds all of my dreams."

The above quote was written during this week in our history by one of the best press agents Estes Park has ever had. The year was 1873, and Isabella Bird was writing one of the many letters to her sister Henrietta ("Hennie") in England that were later published in a book, *A Lady's Life in the Rocky Mountains.*

Since that wonderful volume is readily available in library and bookstore and should be required reading for everyone interested in Estes Park, it will not be quoted again in this article.

Those who have read it no doubt marveled, as I did, at her word-paintings, her uncanny ability to observe and describe in minute detail what she saw. Even after a sleepless night in Longmont and ten hours in the saddle, Miss Bird went on to give a wide-screen account of how and when and what and who she saw as she approached and entered Estes Park for the first time. From mountain trails to Mountain Jim, and from snow in the mountains to snow in her cabin, she graphically continued to tell the story of Estes Park in 1873.

How did she do it? She certainly had a keen mind, but what training did that mind receive?

Isabella Lucy, daughter of Edward and Dora Bird, and named for two grandmothers, was born on October 15, 1831, at Boroughbridge Hall, Yorkshire, England. From the time she was four years old, Isabella was frail and often weak.

To keep her outdoors as much as possible, her father, a minister, sat her on a cushion in front of him as he rode around his parish. Within a couple of years Isabella graduated to her own horse, and as they rode together Mr. Bird would point out everything along the way—the flowers, the animals, the crops, the houses, the businesses, and tell her the uses of all of them. Then he would question her in detail as to what they had seen.

Years later, when asked to what she attributed her gift of observation, Isabella answered "To my father's conversational questioning upon everything."

We thank you, Reverend Bird!

[September 29, 1982]

OCTOBER

Birth of a Valiant Lady

We have mentioned Isabella Bird on other occasions in these writings; when she first came to Estes Park, when she first left, when Mountain Jim died.

For those who may not know, Isabella Bird visited Estes Park in 1873 and wrote letters home to her sister in England, which were eventually published in the book *A Lady's Life in the Rocky Mountains*. It is everyone's reference for life in Estes Park at that time, and is available in libraries, bookstores, and from the University of Oklahoma Press at Norman.

Now that we've made our plug, and everyone either has read or will read Miss Bird's book, we can get on with telling a little bit about her life away from Estes Park, and some things that are not in her book.

Isabella Lucy, daughter of Edward and Dora Bird, and named for two grandmothers, was born on October 15, 1831, at Boroughbridge Hall, Yorkshire, England.

Because of ill health when she was very small, Isabella's doctor suggested that to keep her in fresh air her father, a minister, should take her along on his rides around his parish. From him she learned observation, memory, and the names, habits, and uses of flowers and plants. She learned to ride at an early age, was always fearless and never lacked the ability to speak her mind.

The Bird children were taught by their mother, and Miss Bird's biographer wrote, "To be in the open air, to be with her parents, to understand therefore almost unconsciously the conditions of life and human intercourse, the arts too of speaking, reading, and writing; to absorb from father and mother opinions, standards, tastes, and distastes—these were her education in the truest sense."

When she was eighteen years old Isabella was very ill and needed surgery. "Of the operation itself no record remains, beyond the fact that a fibrous tumor was removed from the neighbourhood of the spine. In after years she was subject to long periods of suffering in that region of her back."

For the next six summers the Birds spent several weeks in the Scottish Highlands. Of these times, and of her father, Miss Bird wrote, "He loved Scotland, not more for its beauty than for its hallowed Sabbaths and Christian zeal and for the love with which he was ever welcomed by his Presbyterian brothers."

Such was Isabella's early life, and such were some of the influences upon it.

During one of the above-mentioned summers, 1854, she was not with the family in Scotland. Her health had deteriorated, and the doctor urged a sea voyage. His prescription was filled when Mr. Bird gave Isabella a hundred pounds and "leave to stay away as long as it lasted."

She took the Canada, a royal mail steamer of the Cunard line, to Halifax, Nova Scotia, in early summer. In August she went by steamer, coach and train to Boston, then to Cincinnati. She then "crossed the prairies to Chicago."

On the train between Rock Island and Chicago a man

sat next to her in the car. "She felt his hand in her pocket abstracting her purse, in which there was only enough money for petty travelling needs, but which contained her luggage checks. She sat passive, giving no indication of her loss till the luggage checks were being collected. When the official reached her, she bowed politely towards her neighbour and said, 'This gentleman has my checks,' and he was startled into giving them up."

From Chicago she went by rail and steamer to Toronto and stopped on the way in Detroit.

She almost drowned when a steamer tipped in Lake Ontario. She spent a month in the back country of Canada. After her return to Toronto she went on to Niagara. "She devoted many pages of her letters home to this last experience, which she 'did' to the bitter end, to Termination Rock, '230 ft. behind the Great Horseshoe Fall,' as was stated on her certificate."

She went down the St. Lawrence to the Thousand Islands and cruised among them. She "shot the rapids at a rate of twenty-five miles an hour next morning when it was daylight, and so reached Montreal."

She went on to Quebec where "One of her most interesting new acquaintances was Dr. Mountain, the Protestant Bishop of Quebec; famous for his arduous journeys to the Red River Settlements in a canoe, for the purpose of confirming 864 Indian converts, and ordaining two of their missionaries."

Then back to Montreal, on to New York and Boston and a "return to Halifax in the Cunard steamer America to join seven of her relatives, the Swabeys, bent on going back to England."

The cruise home was pleasant and uneventful, and

"She reached her home after seven months' absence, with ten pounds of the original 100 pounds in her pocket—better in health, full of animation, and devoutly thankful to be once more with her parents and sister in the peaceful rectory of Wyton."

So ended Miss Bird's first trip abroad. She now had a taste of extended travel, and it must have been palatable, for there was much to follow.

[October 5, 1983]

Isabella Bird's Worldly Travels

Isabella Bird wrote the book *A Lady's Life in the Rocky Mountains.* It focuses on the Estes Park area, but last week we started to tell some of Miss Bird's life away from the Rocky Mountains. Let's continue.

While she was on her trip to North America her family saved all of her letters, and "in her notebooks were statistics and deductions most studiously collected and recorded. Her father urged her to revise these ample materials and give them literary form."

She spent five months of 1855 performing that task. Anna Stoddart, Miss Bird's biographer, wrote, "It was not difficult; for the letters narrated every day's doings and impressions, and were full of vivacious description. Besides, she loved writing for its own sake, and use and study had developed her natural facility of expression."

For all of her achievements and abilities, Miss Bird was a modest lady, as noted in the letter she wrote to her publisher on October 1, 1855:

"I have prepared for the press some travels in the United States, Canada, and the eastern Colonies in North America, taken in the summer, autumn, and winter of last year. The title is *The Car and the Steamboat,* and I, or rather some literary friends whom I have consulted, think that there is sufficient of novelty in them to justify their publication."

The manuscript was accepted, but with the

suggestion that the title be changed to *The Englishwoman in America*. Miss Bird did not really like the change but went along with it even though she considered it "too pretentious for a young authoress."

The book was well accepted on both sides of the Atlantic, and Isabella Bird was well on her way to becoming a well-known traveler and author.

In 1857, Isabella's health failed again, and her doctor urged her to take another trip to America. She planned on being gone six months, but it was almost a year before the journey ended.

No book was written about her second trip, but an 1858 letter gives a brief summary. Considering the extension of U.S. settlement after 1858, a section of that letter might be of interest: "six weeks in making a tour of the far, far west—over the prairies of Illinois and Wisconsin, forty miles beyond railroads, up the Upper Mississippi, into the Minnesota Territory, to the falls of Minnehaha, up Lake Huron and to the extreme end of Lake Superior, and into the Hudson's Bay Territory among the wild Indians."

She went about 2,000 miles on that swing, and had very little stationary time—"frequent change was the most likely to benefit my health."

In 1859, her book *Religion in America* was published.

1860: "Miss Bird was in those years often suffering from spinal prostration, and could seldom rise before noon.

"She wrote propped up by pillows, a flat writing-board upon her knees, and letters or sheets of manuscript scattered around her."

From 1862 to 1866 Isabella purchased many

passages for emigrants to Canada or the United States, and furnished them with clothes and other supplies.

In July of 1870 Isabella was at home, frail and in pain. "Dr. Noir suggested a steel net to support her head at the back when she required to sit up, her suffering being caused by the weight of head on a diseased spine."

On July 11, 1872, she left Edinburgh for Australia, and reached Melbourne on October 5. On November 28 Isabella boarded a small steamer and went to New Zealand, where she stayed until January 1, 1873. She then left for the Sandwich Islands, reaching Honolulu on January 25.

Miss Bird's stay in what is now the State of Hawaii is described in her book *Six Months in the Sandwich Islands*.

As we all know from reading *A Lady's Life in the Rocky Mountains*, her health improved, and Isabella made her way across the United States from west to east, with an extended stay in Estes Park. While here this 42-year-old lady, whose spine would hardly support her head, rode hundreds of miles on horseback and climbed Longs Peak, or was "dragged up, like a bale of goods" by Mountain Jim Nugent in October of 1873.

Back to England she went, and over the years had many, many more experiences:

1878–79: Japan, China, Malay Peninsula, Egypt. She fulfilled a desire and camped on the "solemn slope of Mount Sinai" for four days.

On March 8, 1881 Isabella Bird and Dr. John Bishop were married at the little church of St. Lawrence, Barton-on-the-Heath, in Warwickshire.

On March 6, 1886 Dr. Bishop died after a long illness.

More travel: Europe, Egypt, Holy Land, India, Tibet, Persia, Tangier, Japan, Korea, China.

Then missionary work and more writing—books, articles.

In May of 1900, Mrs. Bishop wrote, "I have begun French conversation lessons, lessons in photography (developing, platinotyping, and lantern-slide making by reduction), and am preparing to take a few cooking lessons."

She made more travels to Africa and Gibraltar and rode horseback from Marrakech to Tangier amidst warring tribes.

Back to England for lectures, more writing, and more health problems.

We have covered a lot of Mrs. Bishop's life, but not much of this column has been devoted to Estes Park history the past two weeks. However, since Miss Bird has been quoted so often regarding a few months of our history, I thought you might like to know a little more about her.

Last week we told of her birth, which was during *this* week of our history.

Today we must report that during *last* week in our history, October 7, 1904, Isabella Lucy Bird Bishop said, "Pray that I may have an abundant entrance."

Then her spirit fled.

[October 12, 1983]

Gentlemen Are Born, Not Made

Longmont, Colorado was the meeting place for a young man from Fairfield County, Ohio and a couple from Estes Park. Mr. and Mrs. William James had spent the winter there, and it was early summer, 1889, when John Adams asked them for a job.

Johnny arrived in Estes Park on July 11 to begin his duties at the Elkhorn Lodge, and in her memoirs Eleanor Hondius, daughter of Mr. and Mrs. James, stated that Johnny Adams was a stableboy. In a letter to his brother Jerry, of Lyons, Kansas, Johnny wrote: "I take care of the horses and wash dishes and a little of everything now. But I can do it. There are no flies on me."

That letter, dated September 18, 1889, also revealed that Johnny wasn't too sure of his future at that time: "Well I am still at the park in the same place but it is not likely that I will be here much longer as there are but six boarders and some of them are going away this week. There are but two boarding horses now besides his own and they are going away on Friday and it is quite likely that I will not be needed much longer...when you write your next letter address it to the Park and if I should not be here I will have it sent to where I am."

Even though his future was uncertain, Johnny wasn't too worried about it: "I can get jobs I think plenty but I want to suit myself a little if I can I don't want to be every body's lacky."

I never had the pleasure of knowing Mr. Adams, but

from all I've read and heard, the above quote tells a lot about him. He was willing to do anything for anyone, to help his friends and community, and he considered all others his equal as human beings.

Eleanor Hondius also wrote, "Whenever Mr. Hondius was lonely or restless, he would go to the village, buy a basket of grapes or a bag of peanuts, go get Johnny, and the two of them would spend the day together. Although Mr. Hondius was a highly educated man, and Johnny had little formal education, the two were fast friends and had much in common."

By the way, Johnny didn't leave the Park in 1889.

Early in 1900 Mr. Adams homesteaded on Fall River a few miles above the Elkhorn Lodge, and he always walked to the village for supplies and newspapers.

One time Mrs. Stanley invited Johnny to her home for dinner. When Mrs. Hondius asked her about the dinner a few days later she replied, "Mr. Adams was just the same in my drawing room as when I talk to him in the village." The thoughts of Mrs. Hondius were "gentlemen are born and not made, and Johnny was a gentleman."

She also described him as "a quiet man, a kind man, and an incessant reader."

Johnny sold all of his land but two acres, on which he built a new cabin with a living room, kitchen, and screened-in utility porch.

Mrs. Hondius wrote, "I had only given one 'shower,' and that was for a bride-to-be. I thought it would be a good idea to give a shower for Johnny Adams, a bachelor, although I had some trouble persuading him that it was the thing to do." They furnished him with a kitchen sink, kitchen linoleum, dishes, cutlery, cooking utensils, table and chairs, bedding, and a table for his books.

"We dressed Johnny's cabin up so nicely we decided to do away with the housewarming for fear some designing woman might try to acquire Johnny and his new abode, and undo all the good we had tried to do for him."

Johnny was not considered a "ladies' man," and he never married, but let's remember what the West was like when it and he were young. I don't think he would mind if we quote a little more of his 1889 letter: "I was only up here a month and I could go out with the best girl on the ranch Geo. has been out here over a year and I don't believe He had a holt of a girl. I can go with any of them but I don't want too there are some of the d-mst hardest girls and women and men out here you ever saw as deceitful as the devil himself but I know it I am no spring chicken if my feathers are short."

George was John's brother, born January 6, 1866, and Johnny was born this week in our history on October 17, 1867. They were the eighth and ninth of ten children in the family. George came to the Park later, and homesteaded not far from Johnny, near where Nicky's Restaurant is now.

For two or three winters in the early days of Estes Park a group known as the Literary Society of Estes Park met at the schoolhouse. Johnny Adams was president.

In 1926 the Women's Club was beautifying the town park and "John Adams, who is especially successful in such work, has consented to transplant some of the Colorado silver spruce to the park." This was just one example of his many contributions to the Town.

Another 1926 report in the *Trail* stated that Johnny had made his first trip to the valley in twelve years, having been called for jury duty.

"Mr. Adams noted many changes and improvements all along the way... he had the privilege of riding from Loveland to Fort Collins over the first stretch of paved road he has ever seen in the state."

Mr. Hondius had built a six-mile pipeline from upper Beaver Meadows, which Mrs. Hondius inherited. She had to furnish water to 150 summer cottages, and Johnny Adams took care of the pipeline for her. Mrs. Hondius remarked that "several times at 10 or 11 o'clock at night, I would have to go get Johnny and take him to the Beaver to run down the person or persons who were draining our pipeline."

A 1950 article observed that, "After 61 years John Adams can truly call himself a native of Estes Park. Johnny can usually be seen at Brodie Brothers Market and has become quite well known among both temporary and permanent residents in the area."

On this anniversary of his birth it seemed right that some of us who weren't here then should also know just a little about a "born gentleman."

John Adams died on March 11, 1953, at the age of 86.

[October 19, 1983]

How the Museum Evolved

At their regular meeting on October 22, 1962, the Town Board approved land in the northwest corner of Stanley Park as the location of a building for the Estes Park Area Historical Museum.

Henry Dannells was the museum's representative at that meeting, and reported that a small building was planned—one that could be added to when need and finances warranted.

Since that meeting was during this week in our history, it gives me an opportunity to pass along a few facts about the museum.

Earlier that year the Chamber of Commerce called a meeting to see if there was enough community interest to form a society to collect, preserve, and display Estes Park artifacts. On May 9, Harold Alps, Armie Armstrong, Carl Bailey, Jim Bissell, Jack Coffee, Don Kinney, Ned Linegar, Claire Noyes, Merlin Potts, Dick Statham, and Dave Stirling attended that meeting.

"After discussion... it was informally agreed that an Estes Park Historical and Museum Society should be formed, with area-wide participation, and that it should be a non-profit society," say the minutes.

Jim Bissell was voted temporary chairman.

At the next meeting, on May 17, it was agreed that "...the Society should operate as a separate and completely independent body, and further that all activities include the entire Estes Park area."

Carl Bailey was elected chairman after a motion by Dave Stirling and second by Jack Coffee.

The first official meeting of the Board of Trustees was held on October 11, 1962, at which time it was unanimously agreed that the name of the organization should be Estes Park Area Historical Museum.

We were incorporated on November 13, 1962.

In June 1964, with $3,591.58 in savings and considerable labor and supplies offered as donations, activity began in the northwest corner of Stanley Park, and for the next two years what was lovingly called "The Morgue" took shape.

Finally that first unit was completed, the collected items that had been stored in garages, barns, etc. since 1962 were moved in, and on June 5, 1966, an open house was held.

The museum that had been in gestation for four years now came to life in "The Morgue," with its 20 foot by 40 foot building—the first of more to come.

The second came in 1969, in the form of a 36 foot by 40 foot addition. Five bids had been sent out, two were returned. Both were rejected by the museum as too high, and again donated labor, materials, and funds came to the rescue.

By July 1, the new flag was raised on the new pole, and the new addition was open for visitors.

Ten years later the third room was added. That is another 20 foot by 40 foot addition on the east side of the one built in 1969.

The museum has continued to grow, and although the fourth addition was put on in the spring of 1982, that 20 foot by 20 foot corner does not yet fulfill the need.

But, remember the criterion for adding to the first small building? The need is only half of it.

[October 20, 1982.]

Ferguson, Hubbell First EP Newlyweds

In a place called Otterville, east of Sedalia, Missouri, Horace Ferguson owned and operated a flour mill.

Mr. and Mrs. Ferguson had six children, three boys and three girls. Hunter was the oldest, Anna was next, then Frances (or Fanny), Sally, Horace (or Holly), and James was the baby.

Mrs. Ferguson had suffered long with asthma, so in 1870, on the second trip the Kansas Pacific Railroad made from Kansas City to Denver, she and her husband were on it. Anna wrote, "besides being thrilled with the trip to the 'wild west,' they were very much gratified by the improvement in mother's health."

After advice from the family doctor, Mr. Ferguson closed his mill and joined the St. Louis Colony, which was being formed in St. Louis, Missouri.

That colony settled at Evans, four miles south of Greeley, the year after Greeley was founded. Anna was born on March 18, 1853, so she was 18 years old when the family moved to Colorado in 1871, arriving at Evans on April 23. Mr. Ferguson said, "the only house we could rent was a vacant hotel building, which was a flimsy affair with such a leaky roof that I had to put a tent inside the house to keep my wife dry in her bed."

Five acres of land were included in the ticket when the Fergusons joined the colony, so they built a two-story brick house a mile west of Evans on their tract.

That was their home for two years, during which time Mr. Ferguson invested in cattle just before the hard winter of 1871. "On the 15th of November there came a big storm... from that time until the next May the snow was not off the ground for a day... The cattle drifted everywhere, and many of the cattlemen were reduced to poverty. It took me four years to get back half of mine (94 head, $2,100)."

In '72 he tried to regain a footing with vegetables. "I figured that I had no less than $2,000 right in sight in that garden. Then the grasshoppers came and it was all gone in no time... They had ruined us for that year."

They rented a ranch west of Loveland because the higher altitude helped Mrs. Ferguson, and for the next two years their efforts were again met by clouds of grasshoppers. Also, while they were there, twelve-year-old Holly died of pneumonia.

It was the fall of 1875, "and I was about at my wits end when I read in a Denver paper a letter from the Earl of Dunraven announcing that he had bought Estes Park and warned everybody that he would permit no body there except his guests... somehow I got interested in the place and determined to go up there and take a look around."

Mr. Ferguson and his son Hunter went up and fished and hunted in a virtual paradise. "I saw that there was a chance for a living for me and my family, so I decided to take up a claim and settle in the Park, particularly as my wife's health was always better in the mountains... I picked out this piece (a half-mile north of Mary's Lake) on account of the spring, always being monstrous fond of a good drink of water...

"I'd made up my mind that if I was on land claimed by the English Company I'd fight them and I'd enjoy nothing better than showing them up in the courts. I wasn't going to let them bluff me out of the Park the way I'd seen them do with some of the men. But it turned out when I went to the land office in Denver that the English Company had never filed on my 160 acres at all, so I had no trouble in getting my government title." They built a cabin, and the family moved up.

If you're wondering what all of this has to do with this week in our history, we'll let Anna tell you:

"We built two rooms on the house before we moved in, added two more having a dining room, kitchen, and bed rooms. Also built a cabin or two. This place was known as the Highlands Hotel, and our first boarders were campers. We only served meals, but we built more cottages out from the hotel to rent, and could seat 85 people in the dining room. We had many people from Longmont, Denver, and the East. At the time the Highlands started there were only 2 or 3 places that kept boarders; the Dunraven, the Elkhorn and Sprague's Hotel.

"The McFarlands from Longmont were among our boarders, and I became well acquainted with them. Mrs. McFarland had a number of children, and when I returned from a trip to Denver she persuaded me to help her do some sewing before returning to the Park. It was at her house that I met Mr. Hubbell, who was in business with Mr. McFarland, and a brother of Mrs. McFarland. He took me to the Park when I returned.

"In the fall of 1876 we were married. I recall traveling by wagon from Estes Park to Longmont, then larger than

Denver, and taking the train into Denver to buy my bridal outfit. It was of grey-blue poplin, fashioned with full long sleeves and a high neck. Mr. Hubble wore a black suit.

"There were only a few friends and the family present. That was October 26, 1876, and we were the first couple married in Estes Park. There weren't more than 25 persons in all the Estes Park district, and my wedding was small. The Rev. James Collman, who was pastor of the Methodist church in Longmont, came to the Park to marry us. After the wedding we had a dinner with wedding cake, and everyone stayed over night, even the preacher, for it took a day's traveling to go from Longmont to Estes.

"The next day Mr. Hubbell and I went to Longmont, where he owned and managed a general store. Before we were married he gave me a lovely broach which was made of Colorado gold and moss agate. If we had lived in Estes Park we would have had to buy our household supplies in Longmont, for those were the days before a general store was opened, and some time before the first school in the district started.

"Oscar, Dick, Horace, and Hervey were all born in Longmont. In 1891 we moved to Berthoud where Mr. Hubbell operated another business. John and Betty were born there, and in 1900 we moved to Fort Collins, where Mr. Hubbell retired. He wrote his "Personal Reminiscences" of the Civil War, which was published in a newspaper in Richmond, Missouri. He was a member of the Masonic Lodge, and I was a member of the Eastern Star."

[October 26, 1983]

NOVEMBER

Community Church of Rockies Moves—But Not Too Quickly

The *Estes Park Trail* (newspaper) has a lot of similarities to the Estes Park Trails (the dirt and rock kind). Some are tedious, some are boring, on some the view is fascinating and spectacular, and always there are surprises.

One of the surprises that I found while hiking in an *Estes Park Trail* from this month in our history was that: "The Sunday traffic during the summer season has become so tremendous that the present location has become somewhat unsatisfactory due to the unavoidable noises of the street and it has also become necessary to consider better accommodations for church services and the Sunday school."

The above quote, and that "At a called meeting of the congregation of the Church Wednesday evening it was decided to obtain a new location" are not actually surprises in themselves.

Neither is the fact that "At the present location traffic is so congested during the summer season that it will very shortly be necessary for the town to restrict parking along Elkhorn Avenue to a short period of time. This would make the present location more unsatisfactory as a church site than ever."

We all know that the Community Church of the Rockies moved from Elkhorn Avenue a couple of years ago. It's no surprise that the above stated reasons are why the church moved.

The surprise was at the top of the page, where it read, "Friday, November 9, 1923."

Yes, sixty-one years ago this month the Community Church decided to move. Two years and three months ago it moved.

What happened to delay a necessary move for almost sixty years? I'm not sure we can fully answer that question, but we can fill in a few things that happened during the three-score-year delay.

Let's move ahead seven months to June 6, 1924, where we read, "Last week a transfer was completed by the trustees of the church whereby the church came into possession of a new building site. Owing to the rapid advance in the value of real estate, the trustees have long felt it imperative to procure additional building space now, instead of waiting until the price became prohibitive. Nine sites were offered for their consideration. The choice of the people was almost unanimous for the property secured. The counsel of the best architects in the state was sought and they declared that property had almost every advantage of an ideal building site, especially in a tourist town. The property purchased is the hillside overlooking the public square between Service's store and the property owned by Mr. Bond. The present small building is being used as a Boy Scout headquarters.

"There is no thought of building at the present time on the new location, or not until the present church property should be sold."

To put that site in present-day familiar surroundings:

The public square is Bond Park, "Service's store" is now the Coffee Bar, and "the small building" is now enlarged and houses the Fisherman's Fly; so picture if you can the Community Church sitting on the hill in place of The Courtyard.

Now let's hike the *Trails* a little more, and rest on April 1, 1932—a mere 50 years before the church moved.

Here we see that "The present church was built soon after the church was organized and is far too small to meet the needs of a growing community. The congregation has plans under way to build a new Sunday school and social unit, which, it is hoped, will be complete this year."

On May 20 we see that "It is proposed to erect the new building on the lots occupied by the present church edifice. At the existing low prices of building materials, the new structure can be completed and equipped for approximately $35,000. In the event a sufficient amount is raised for the entire new building at this time, a religious education and social unit will be constructed at the rear and connected with the present church auditorium, greatly increasing the seating capacity. The unit will be part of the new building when complete, and would cost about $15,000 at the present time."

Three years later the plans had changed, and new plans are announced: "The present church building was built twenty-five years ago, and is far too small for the needs of the community today...

"This addition will consist of: Sunday School auditorium, stage, kitchen, ladies' parlor, pastor's study, a class room for the primary department and a room for the beginners department, janitor's quarters, furnace room, store room, vestibule and coat room, choir and extra Sunday School room."

That addition was built at a cost of fifteen thousand depression dollars and dedicated during week-long festivities from August 18 through August 25, 1935.

Since there are definitely historical events associated with the Community Church of the Rockies in December, I have a good excuse to not ramble on today, and continue this next month.

I'll just mention one other article that was a November item in 1951. On the 23rd we see that the church is alive and well: "With only two dissenting voices, members of the Community Church of the Rockies voted Monday night to go ahead with the remodeling and addition to the structure on Elkhorn Avenue."

Let's take a breather now and hike a few more *Trails* past the church next month.

[November 1984]

Stanley Sale Ended Grand Era

During this week in our history, on October 30, 1922, seventy-two people sat down to an annual Chamber of Commerce banquet at the Stanley Hotel.

Each year the members of the Chamber entertained their ladies with an oyster supper, and again this year "the oysters were fine and done to a queen's taste. Great pains had been taken by Host Lamborn to secure the best for the occasion."

Mr. Lamborn, manager of the Stanley, would not be hosting another oyster supper for the C of C ladies, for he announced during the meal that he would be "severing his connection with the Park, where he had labored the past fourteen years."

He stated that the Stanley Hotel had been sold, and that R.K. Starkweather, former owner of the Savoy Hotel of Denver, had secured it and the ground immediately surrounding it. Also that "Mr. Stanley will probably retain at present his other holdings in the Park."

During my limited research time I searched the subsequent issues of the *Estes Park Trail* for further information regarding a sale of the Stanley Hotel. All I could find in the next couple of months was the following announcement:

"Frank J. Haberl, for thirteen years assistant manager of the Brown Palace hotel and later manager of the Denver Club, has been named as manager of the

Stanley Hotels, says the Denver News. This appointment becomes effective January first.

"Mr. Haberl came to Colorado 21 years ago from Vienna, Austria. His move to the Stanley Hotel will be his third move in nearly a quarter of a century."

I thought I had found something to write about for this week, but with no report of a sale it just sort of fizzled out.

Then, a few years later, on February 5, 1926, a front page headline reads, "Largest Real Estate Deal in History of Estes Park Region Takes Place."

That wasn't during this week in our history, but let's see what it was all about.

"Business circles in Denver and Estes Park were made alert this week when the information leaked out that a deal was being closed for the purchase of Mr. F.O. Stanley's interests in Estes Park for a consideration rumored to exceed a half million dollars.

"The sale is to include all of Mr. Stanley's real estate and personal holdings in Colorado, which includes the Stanley Hotels, the Stanley Power Department and approximately 2,750 acres of land...

"The sale... will make a large and well known eastern hotel company owner of one of the largest and finest tourist hotels in the Rocky Mountain region and the first hotel, it is said, in the country to heat, light and cook meals exclusively with electricity generated by its own hydro-electric plant...

"The company in the deal have not announced themselves and just what they plan to do is not known, nor just the purpose of the purchase.

"Manager Frank J. Haberl, of the Stanley Hotels,

announces that he will remain as manager."

Once again, I searched the subsequent issues of the *Trail*, and found not where "the company in the deal" ever announced themselves. The "well known eastern hotel company" may have been well-known in the East, but I couldn't find them in the *Trail*.

We now progress to find ourselves once again in this week of our history—November 1, 1929. The *Estes Park Trail* of that date has reprinted a story from the *Denver Post*:

"Consolidation of hotels of Estes Park, a million dollar merger, is being planned...

"The deal, which is expected to be consummated in the near future, calls for the consolidation of the Estes Park Chalets and the Stanley Hotels, recently taken into a receivership.

"The Chalets is owned at present by the Rocky Mountain Motor Company and the Stanley is owned by F.O. Stanley, Newton, Mass., famous American inventor...

"It is understood a new company will be formed to take over both hotels, and the management, it is said, will be in the hands of the Rocky Mountain Motor Company, of which Roe Emery is president...

"The merger will bring under one management the two largest hotels in Estes Park."

It must have happened, because in October of 1930, the *Trail* listed real estate transactions of the previous year, and "the greatest transaction, from a monetary standpoint, is the sale of the Stanley Hotel to the Estes Park Hotels Company with Roe Emery as president."

But back to the November 1, 1929 *Trail*, where the

editor, A.B. Harris, wrote a glowing account of Mr. Stanley's life and accomplishments. Perhaps we can end this week's column with the words Mr. Harris used this week in our history in '29 to end his account

"But greater than he anticipated, Mr. Stanley built Estes Park as a great and perpetual monument to himself; for it was his love, foresight and generosity that almost overnight made Estes Park world known.

"Mr. Stanley, Estes Park, yes Colorado, is proud of you! Your memory shall not die. Here, the Stanley Hotel, the community auditorium, the community itself, stand as everlasting monuments perpetuating your memory—memory of a man who would not harm any man, who would not take advantage of the most simple soul, a man whose love and generosity to a community has made it a common name on the lips of an entire nation."
[November 2, 1983]

Local Political Trends

The first week in November has been not only a part of history, but a week in which history was made or altered.

The making of history is not often done with a big bang, a lot of fanfare, or much excitement. Everything we do or say has some effect on someone or something, and we seldom know what that effect is.

This week in our history is slightly different.

Although we still don't know how our words or deeds may have caused someone to vote or not vote, we can see the final results of an election and know if our "x" made any difference.

Let's look back on a few of the elections that have been held in Estes Park.

William H. McCreery (grandfather of Estes Park's present Wm. McCreery) wrote, "At the first general election under Statehood, October 1876, Estes Park proved to be the pivotal precinct. When the returns were all in except Estes Park it seemed that the democratic candidate for State Senator was ahead about three votes, but the small vote of Estes Park (eleven I think) turned the scale and elected Norman H. Meldrum as the first State Senator from Larimer County."

That seemed to be the trend-setter for Estes Park elections. Not that we've always "turned the scale," but check the reasons for that scale-turning. Estes Park has

November 219

usually (but not always) been predominantly Republican, and has usually had a high percentage of voter participation.

In 1922 Estes Park voted Republican about four to one. C.H. Bond had the high vote with 228 of the 250 votes cast for State Representative. For Governor, Griffith had 195 to Sweet's 53 votes. Sweet, a Democrat, won.

In 1924 a record 90 percent of registered voters went to the polls. The turnout was so great that the supply of 350 official ballots furnished by the County Clerk ran out, and eight voters used sample ballots.

Even though Estes Park set some kind of precedent in 1924 by voting more for the person than for the party, and even though William E. Sweet had local ties, his bid for the U.S. Senate in 1926 netted 71 Estes Park votes to the 208 cast for Republican Charles W. Waterman.

The 1926 Governor's race, however, brought the largest Democratic vote ever when William Adams received 135 to Republican Oliver Shoup's 156.

A new record of 413 ballots were cast in 1928 when Estes Park voters scored Herbert Hoover 301 and Alfred E. Smith 101. A strong cross-over vote that year gave 288 votes to Democratic Governor Wm. H. Adams, and 115 to Wm. L. Boatright, his Republican challenger, and Inez Lewis, a Democrat, edged out Katherine Craig for Superintendent of Public Instruction 199 to 184.

The switching around noted in 1928 came forth again in 1932, and shades of 1876, tabulations from precinct 37 decided many county contests. This time the Democrats were the victors.

Joe Mills suggested in 1934 that there was only one

party in Estes Park: the Good Roads Party. This remark prompted about twenty prominent business men to meet on the Sunday night before election to discuss various candidates. After they agreed to support certain ones, a list of the "Estes Park Slate" was printed and passed out on Tuesday.

Every one of those candidates received a majority of votes.

We can go on to tell how the trend toward growth for the Democrats continued, and in 1960 precincts 37 and 37A voted for winners in all state and county races, though they didn't pick the winner between Nixon and Kennedy.

The important thing, however, is that despite a snow storm that year, over 90 percent of the eligible voters again went to the polls.

Maybe a lot of people think Shep Husted is watching. Maybe what he said years ago influenced this week in our history. "Many a man who hasn't time to vote has time to cuss congress."
[November 3, 1982]

Misunderstood Resident Pioneered Propaganda Analysis

He was born in Hanover, Germany on September 22, 1898. From 1912-15 he was a business apprentice; then served in the German Army from 1916–18; was active in the German Revolution in 1918–19, a member of the Constituent Assembly of the Weimar Republic, 1918; Editor and Publisher, *Die Filmwoche,* Berlin, from 1919-1925.

After coming to the United States in 1926, he was a factory worker in Detroit and Chicago, then a radio engineer in 1927–28.

From 1928 through 1932 he was a reporter and assistant editor of the Chicago *Abendpost.* From 1932 to 1935 he was American correspondent for Vienna daily newspapers, and for the next three years was a freelance writer.

On October 18, 1935, he married Winnifred S. Sparks, and in 1937 became a naturalized citizen.

In 1940, and again in 1942, he was elected Justice of the Peace in Allenspark, Colorado. We could try to research his activities while JP in Allenspark, but there are parts of Siegfried "Sig" Wagener's life that go well beyond that position.

On October 10, 1939, daily columns entitled "We're Listening—War on Air Waves" began appearing in the *Chicago Times* under the name B.E. Lucas.

Mr. Wagener was listening to shortwave Nazi propaganda broadcasts, analyzing them, and writing about them under an assumed name to protect his mother in Berlin and his sister in Vienna. The name he had assumed was his mother-in-law's maiden name, and "my column had appeared but a few weeks when first the German Consul General sniffed me out from undercover. Thereafter all hell broke loose...

"My sister, a well-known Viennese actress, was several times interrogated by the Gestapo. They tried to put the screws on her for what her brother was doing to Nazi propaganda in America."

He moved his listening post to Tahosa Valley in 1940, "mainly because it is our home and secondarily for better short-wave reception."

This German-born citizen got his high-powered radio sets operating at 9000 feet, and continued to listen, to analyze, to write. He also had a twice-weekly broadcast, "Analysis of Propaganda," over 120 network stations of the Mutual Broadcasting System.

In 1946 he wrote, "Today I take pride in the fact that I was the first who pioneered for the most essential anti-propaganda work. Quite naturally, I had to take the kicks to which the breeches of every pioneer are exposed."

Many of those "kicks" were the result of suspicion by people in the area who thought he was a Nazi agent.

"One of the Denver FBI boys dropped in to talk over some cases on which I had collaborated with the Department of Justice. After we were through with the job he leaned back.

"'Now, Mr. Wagener, we know you are a friend of ours

and I hate to tell you this. But people are running us ragged with denunciations about you and I wish you would give me all the data about yourself so we can answer them properly.'"

Many continued to think of him as a spy, and rumors were plentiful.

"There was the rumor about my workmen and ranch hands being my bodyguards armed and trigger-happy at all times, and ably assisted by my pack of 'man- killing' dogs...

"There was that fanciest of all fancy rumors of Michael Marden, miles away and out of sight, signaling me with his porch light, 'that a Nazi plane would land in the night,' while my good friend Stu Gore was allegedly an FBI agent watching me...

"But then when you find unsolicited letters of praise from President Roosevelt and other people of consequence in your fan mail... you know it was worth it...

"When I started it in January 1939, no American newspaper and radio commentator would touch the subject of Axis shortwave propaganda with a ten-foot pole.

"When I switched off my receivers for the last time in September 1943, everybody in press and radio was deep in analyzing and fighting Axis shortwave propaganda."

Besides his column and broadcasts, Mr. Wagener furnished analytical information to the Department of State, War Department, Federal Communications Commission, Coordinator of Information and other government agencies before the government established its own listening posts in 1942.

Again in 1946, Wagener wrote, "The predictions which I culled from the world's shortwave propaganda right here in the shadow of Longs Peak read today like the roster of the war's major events, foreseen and put on public record sometimes years before they actually took place."

In 1943 he signed on with the Office of Strategic Services, and during the next eighteen months served the OSS evaluating (this time) the U.S. efforts in political and psychological warfare in the European Theatre of Operations.

After the war, "Sig" Wagener returned to the Allenspark area, invested in real estate, and became owner of the Tahosa Valley Land Office.

His wife, Winnie, died July 19, 1971, and during this week in our history, on November 26, 1976, Siegfried "Sig" Wagener, perhaps one of the most misunderstood residents of the area at one time, also departed this life. [November 23, 1983]

Thanksgiving Homestead

During this week in our history there was a house warming two miles on the Allenspark side of Longs Peak Inn, and the first entry in the guest register was made by the famous owner of that famous Inn.

"Enos A. Mills, Longs Peak—The best lighted and the warmest Beaver House that I have seen" was his inscription and description for the brand-new homestead cabin of Katherine Griffith Garetson.

The others who came on November 22, 1914, to warm that house and to wish well its hostess signed in the following order: John Dickinson Sherman, Mrs. Will H. Lamb and Margaret, Alfred Oberg, Mary G. Rockwell, Julian S. Johnson, Nettie M. Rockwell, Annie Adele Shreve, Charles C. Hanscom.

The last entry for that day states, "When the cool of night came down the house had been warmed. (Thank the Lord the warming's over!) Katherine G. Garetson."

The next page, for Thanksgiving, 1914, is signed by Alfred Oberg, Enos A. Mills, Charles C. Hanscom, John Dickinson Sherman, Annie Adele Shreve, Katherine G. Garetson (Homesteader), and Miss Gypsy Dane (her mark) X.

Such was the beginning of homestead life for a lady from St. Louis, her friend and companion, A.A. Shreve, and her two hundred-plus pound Great Dane, Gypsy.

"Filing a three-year residence claim is the most

serious thing you can do, aside from marrying, I think. The more I thought, the more I feared," Miss Garetson later wrote.

In spite of her fears and the seriousness of the undertaking, she had located the quarter section she wanted, gone to the land office in Denver, filled out the papers, sworn an oath, paid $16 in fees, and became a homesteader.

While her cabin was being built Katherine lived at her sister's summer cottage near Longs Peak Inn with "A.A." and Gypsy.

They became well acquainted with Enos Mills and Alfred Oberg, who worked with him, and Katherine wrote, "Alfred had much concern over my preparations for the winter, and Mr. Mills, while pretending it was a matter-of-fact thing for a woman to brave a Rocky Mountain winter, must have been aghast at times over the foolhardiness of my exploit. Nothing would have induced me to go into that undertaking had I known what things could happen; what the life was like."

Space does not allow me to tell in detail what did happen, or what life was like, but consider this partial list:

Snow, ice, coyotes, mountain lions

Smoke and freezing temperatures in the house from cold stoves due to pitch not cleaned from stoves and chimneys

Monotony

Clearing the land—sawing and splitting logs

Spring thaw, with flooded store room

After the first winter, "It is worthwhile to have had to chop ice, shovel snow, carry water up hill, bring in all the fuel from the outside, saw frozen beef into steaks; wash, iron, scrub, and break through two and a half miles of snow to get the mail carrier's burden"

Plant a crop

Rats, mice, chipmunks, flies

During the first year the road they were on was moved a quarter of a mile, so the new business they were starting was on an abandoned road

Discouraging comments from others

Dog problems—dog had to go

Debts

Friend and companion left to teach school

Alone—loneliness, tired, beaten, necessities neglected, talking to self

More rats and mice

Patrons had to park half a mile up the road and walk

Crops didn't come up

Ran out of fire wood

Clock froze solid

Long, long winter

Ran out of food

Finally, "My three years would be up on the twentieth of November. Then I would notify the land office that I had completed my term of residence, and would go down with two witnesses to 'prove up."

But, after three years of struggle, her right to a patent was contested by the Forest Service, and it took almost two more years before she held in her hand that precious document with Woodrow Wilson's signature.

Many years earlier, as a guest of Longs Peak Inn, Katherine Garetson had visited the beaver colonies west of what became her homestead.

When she filed for her claim she remembered shivering away the sunset, eating cold lunches in a vain attempt to see the beaver at work, and vowed to have a tea room where others could have a hot supper within a ten minute walk from those colonies.

Big Owl Tea Place, named that first Thanksgiving almost five years earlier, along with Big Owl Hill were now hers.

As Enos Mills said when she opened the envelope from Washington, "Indeed, you have earned your patent!"

[November 24, 1982]

Buel Porter's Christmas Legacy

During this week in our history for about the last thirty years, Estes Park residents and visitors have enjoyed the work of Buel Porter.

His larger-than-life artwork can be seen in various parts of Estes Park. "Shepherds, watching their flocks by night" are also looking skyward with wonder at a special glow. Wisemen are following a special star. Santa Claus is skimming along a bluff, on his way to special children. "Christmas in Bugville" tells a special story of its own. Nearby, a Nativity scene tells another special story; and high on a rocky hill, a Christ figure looks down on a special town.

The Park's own Christmas artist was born on January 22, 1896 in Quincy, Illinois. Rather than waiting until that week to tell about him, it seemed more appropriate to use one of the weeks that his art is on display—here for all to view during the season that many celebrate the birth of another, two thousand years ago.

Mr. Porter's early days were spent as an auto mechanic and welder in his father's machine shop.

Later, while serving in the Army during World War I, an injury caused loss of hearing, so he was released from active duty. The government gave him two years of rehabilitation training so he could support himself with his hearing disability.

Porter's livelihood then came as a sign painter and

theatre lobby artist. He became one of the best, earning double the average pay for the times.

He at one time was in charge of the art department at the Kansas City Slide Co. in Kansas City, Missouri.

While in Kansas City, doing the lobby art for all of the city's Fox Theatres, Porter knew another young artist who was getting his start as a cartoonist. Walt Disney went on to other things.

The Porter family went on to other things, too. In June 1951, they moved to Estes Park, where he began by painting signs.

Shortly after moving here, he made a Santa with sleigh and reindeer for the roof of a house at Christmas time. Mrs. Roberta Porter recalls that the Quota Club used it the next year in Bond Park.

Porter learned that the town was looking for a Christmas display, so he offered to make Estes Park a nationally known Christmas season town for about one third of the usual cost. He agreed to do the displays for an average of $300 each. He estimated that the cost could have averaged $1,000.

By 1955 a much larger Santa was there—flying above the bluff, much as theology professor Clement Moore must have pictured him in 1822 when he wrote a poem for his children, "A Visit from St. Nicholas" ("'Twas the Night Before Christmas").

The Nativity scene was also among the first of Porter's many Christmas creations.

Some of his work had been over 60 feet high. The Christ figure is 22 feet tall, and the shepherds are "three times as high as the ceiling in an average house"—24 feet! For the figures to be noticed from a distance such size was necessary.

The 1969 Vacation Edition of the *Estes Park Trail* tells some of the secrets for Porter's larger-than-life art:

"He started by going to his 'morgue,' a file of ideas and pictures, for inspiration. Once he had visualized the scene he desired, he made a hand drawing of it on an approximate scale of one inch to each foot of the size he wished the final product to be.

"Utilizing an overhead projector Porter blew up the drawing to actual size, projecting blocks of it at a time on four-foot by eight-foot paper panels.

"Then, with a rolling perforator, he outlined the projected image on the paper with uniformly placed holes, actually tracing the line-drawing upon the paper.

"Next, he attached the paper to white painted wood boards and powdered the paper with a black powder which adhered to the board, beneath the holes.

"When he removed the paper the powder showed the outline of the projected figure on the wood. Porter then connected the dots of powder with a pencil.

"A hand held jig saw, called a 'cutawl' was then brought into play to cut the excess wood from the outline of the figure.

"The painting of the figure followed, taking up the bulk of the time spent on the project. The entire job often took up to a month, Porter explains."

Santa's Christmas Card Studio and the Nativity Scene required the longest and most detailed painting.

Regarding the painting and the colors, Porter said, "Color to me is like music, the end result must be perfect rhythm. And the mood while I am painting takes on great importance."

When he was 72 years old, he remarked, "I put a lot of enthusiasm into my work because I think Christmas is a special time, especially for little kids... I can still remember believing in Santa Claus for so long that I was ashamed when someone told me he didn't exist."

Mr. Porter's wife, Roberta, was a long-time employee of the town and still lives in Estes Park. His son, Bob, is president of The Estes Park Bank; and a daughter, Barbara Ann Souther, lives in Aurora.

Buel Franklin Porter died in Estes Park on July 7, 1969, but Christmas as a "special time" lives on in Estes Park.

[November 30, 1983]

DECEMBER

Twists of History Led to Library

"The ladies' auxiliary of the Estes Park Protective and Improvement Association and the officers of the Business Men's Association met at Clatworthy's store on Monday evening to discuss ways and means of raising funds for the purpose of improving the roads and trails of the Park."

The above quote from the June 29, 1912, *Estes Park Trail* is followed by an editorial in the July 27 edition which begins, "The entertainments given by the residents of the Park, to raise money for roads and trails, are most commendable and should receive the most liberal patronage."

On August 3, 1912, a leap year dance at Elkhorn Lodge is described in the *Trail*, and the story ends:

"This brilliant function was given for the benefit of the roads and trails fund—a very worthy cause.

"It will be a consolation to all those who could not attend to learn there will be several opportunities for them to contribute to this fund."

What does this fund-raising effort in the summer of 1912 have to do with this week in our history?

Let's see what Eleanor Hondius of Elkhorn Lodge had to say in her Memoirs.

"That summer, we decided to raise money for roads and trails; and because a group of men in the community known as the Businessmen's association had the same goal, we combined forces and held a dance every two weeks at a different hotel.

"I went to the last meeting of the Protective Society to hand over the $300 to $400 we had raised that summer. I was told it was kind of us to have raised the money, but we were only an Auxiliary, and could not dictate to the Association the use of the money. I refused to hand over the money.

"A few weeks later, the women met at the Hupp Hotel and formed a society known as the Woman's Club, which has been in existence since. The money went into our own treasury."

No, the founding of the Woman's Club isn't what we are remembering this week, but we're getting closer.

Although it was no longer an auxiliary, the Woman's Club became an improvement association of its own.

Among their accomplishments in 1913 were the purchase of a sprinkling cart to keep the dust down on Elkhorn Avenue, the completion of the trail to the summit of Deer Mountain, and the appointment of a committee to select a library site.

Now we come to Alma Bond's account of the actions of the Woman's Club about three years later.

"The Club voted to use the interest on Building Fund ($50.00) and one-third of the annual dues (which would be about $60.00) for the support of a library.

"The committee was asked to make the following proposition to the School Board: That the Club would care for the school library if they would give them a room in the school house for a library two afternoons a week; the board agreed to this, and on December 1, 1916, The Woman's Club Library was opened, with Florence Bond as librarian at a salary of $1.50 per week."

Florence was the daughter of Alma and Cornelius H. Bond. She was graduated from Estes Park High School in 1917.

Florence was librarian for the next 25 years, and during that time the library grew.

In 1922 the Town provided a lot in the park that was later named in honor of C.H. Bond, and a library building was erected. The name was changed to The Estes Park Library.

In 1935 Eleanor Hondius presented a memorial to her husband, Pieter, an addition that doubled the size and efficiency of the library.

Strange and interesting twists emerge when you stir around in history. I wonder what kind of library we would have now if Eleanor Hondius had turned over the fund-raising effort of the Ladies' Auxiliary to the Protective and Improvement Association in 1912, and if the Woman's Club had not been formed...

Oh, by the way—the treasurer of the Estes Park Protective and Improvement Association in 1912 was Pieter Hondius, and C.H. Bond was its secretary.
[December 1, 1982]

The Secret to Shaping Young Minds

"When once china or porcelain has been inscribed, and put into a furnace, and baked and glazed, you cannot rub the inscription off. It is too late then. If you want to rub it off, you must do it while the ware is in the 'biscuit.'

"When children come into our hands, they are in the 'biscuit,' and we can inscribe on them what we please."   **Henry Ward Beecher**

The above quote was found on page 137 of a small book called *Stories for Talks to Boys*.

The 356 pages of that book are filled with quotes from famous and not-so-famous people, from newspapers and other publications.

The table of contents covers two-and-one-half pages with subjects from Action, Aim or Purpose, and Ambition through Bravery, Cigarettes, Conceit, Courtesy, Duty, Failure, Honesty, Ideals, Optimism, Perseverance, Procrastination, Sacrifice, and Service, to Thrift, Vision, Willpower, and Work.

This sampling of subject headings could give you an idea that the person who compiled the book had certain character values shared by many famous and not-so-famous people.

His life's work consisted of inscribing those values on children placed into his hands in the biscuit state.

After his special method of baking and glazing, the inspiration of Frank Cheley didn't rub off.

Who was Frank Cheley, and what was that special method?

Frank Howbert Cheley was born in Colorado Springs in 1889. He grew up there, went through high school there, and attended Colorado College there. He also worked with the Colorado Springs YMCA.

YMCA work took him to South Bend, Indiana, where he became the director of their summer camp at Three Rivers, Michigan. He went to the St. Louis "Y" and operated a camp for them in the Ozarks for a time. Then back to Denver to the Olinger Highlander Boys, the YMCA again, and Scouting.

Mr. Cheley edited two 20-volume sets of books called "The Father and Son Library" and "Modern Boy Activity."

The books were intended to help parents and children with the concept of family fun and family learning.

He later published an additional 43 volumes related to children, camping, nature, and so on.

Frank's son, Jack, said, "I think the best way to size up my dad's philosophy is to say that he felt there was a need to help boys grow into manhood through the experiences of the great outdoors.

"He was convinced that to make the most of such an experience young people need to be associated with the right kind of adult leaders."

In 1921, Frank Cheley leased some land at Bear Lake from the National Park Service and started his own camp. It was called The Bear Lake Trail School—An Alpine Summer Camp for Boys.

The first season there were nine campers, and the

second there were 13.

By 1926 the capacity at Bear Lake was 60 boys.

Of that same year Jack tells us, "My dad's ideas had grown and developed to the point where he felt there was a need for a girls' camp."

That camp, near the YMCA of the Rockies, was called "Camp Chipeta, a vigorous camp for vigorous girls." The name of the Ute Indian Chief Ouray's wife was Chipeta.

Both camps grew, then split into age groups. There was a need for separate camps for separate ages.

"So, it came about that one of the finest timbered canyons in the whole region of Rocky Mountain National Park, six miles from the village of Estes Park on the main Longs Peak road, was secured; and two new camps were built, one on either side of the valley, built of native stone and logs.

"Lodges, dining rooms, sleeping cabins, the very best water supplied by a springfed stream—all just one mile off the main-traveled road. This 160 acres that became our original camp land was purchased from Ted Jelsema."

Then came the Depression.

Jack said, "If any of you remember 1932 very well, we had more staff than we had campers, and my dad didn't have the heart to fire them. So he made a deal.

"He said, 'You can stay and eat, but you don't get any pay. If you want to go somewhere else where you can get a job, go to it.' Many of the staff stayed through 1932."

Things did pick up again, though, and more expansion occurred.

The first "Girls' Trail's End Ranch" is at the end of Fox Creek, and the "Boys' Trail's End" is up Dunraven

Glade on the North Fork of the Thompson.

What is now known as Cheley Colorado Camps has a staff of over 75, serves close to 800 children a season, and consists of 395 acres at the main camp south of Estes Park, 80 acres at each of the Trail's End Ranches, another 80 acres below Charles Eagle Plume's on Big Owl Road, and 160 acres east of Little Valley used for camping and outdoor education.

Jack tells us that the camp "in a sense provides for physical, mental, spiritual, and social growth. All of the facets that it takes for each of those particular things are necessary for a young boy or a young girl to grow, mature, and develop."

That's not too different from H.W. Beecher's definition of education that Frank Cheley included in the book we quoted at the beginning—"Education is the knowledge of how to use the whole of oneself.

"Men are often like knives with many blades; they know how to open one and only one; all the rest are buried in the handle, and they are no better than they would have been if they had been made of but one blade.

"Many men use but one or two of the faculties with which they have been endowed. A man is educated who knows how to make a tool of every faculty, how to open it, how to keep it sharp, and how to apply it to all practical purposes."

Frank Cheley, the man who was always called "The Chief," whose philosophy was to help boys and girls open every blade, and who inspired them to learn by doing, and to do so with character, died during this week in our history—December 17, 1941.

[December 14, 1983]

Early Electrical Woes

A short notice in the December 16, 1921 *Estes Park Trail* states, "Low water pressure and heavy use of current for heating reduced the power so that the motors in the *Trail* office wouldn't turn—result, the *Trail* didn't get into the mails until Saturday afternoon."

Ironically, just three months earlier they had run a story about a "...new big generator purchased at a cost of $17,000...

"The generator will be installed in October at the close of the tourist season and will more than double the capacity of the plant and supply all the power in the Park for years to come."

In the December 2 edition, two short weeks before our week in history, we read, "Estes Park has one of the finest power plants in the west and in addition to this there are a number of individual plants, many of them being driven by water power, and others by gasoline or kerosene engines."

No, I'm not getting ready to bad-mouth the *Trail* or the power plant. The *Trail* merely stated facts, that the Fall River Power Plant was one of the best systems going, but they did have a problem getting the paper out this week in 1921.

So, if we keep reading, a year and a week later we find out what was done to correct the situation.

"During the past summer F.O. Stanley, owner of the

power plant, spent almost his entire time and many thousands of dollars in improving the plant. A new pipe line had been laid a year or two previously and last season a new dam was built at the entrance to Horseshoe Park that insured a better volume of water and so constructed that ice would not so greatly hamper the operation of the plant. A new power line from the plant to the village was also built at considerable outlay."

Mr. Stanley first came to Estes Park in 1903, and among his many accomplishments was the establishment of the power plant on Fall River which began operation in 1908.

Nothing I've written about today happened during this week in our history, except that the newspaper was late. It was late because of power failure, due to low water on a hydro-electric system. That prompted the building of a dam.

While we're at it, let's put out a couple more dates that aren't during this week either.

Am I mistaken, or did I see in the August 27, 1982, *Trail-Gazette* a series of five photographs taken by Grace David George and her daughter Jennifer showing Cascade Dam being destroyed during the July 15 Lawn Lake Flood?

The power plant also received extensive damage on July 15.

[December 15, 1982]

A Guide for All Seasons

Edna Ferber, the novelist, came to Estes Park in the early 1900s for the first time. She was fascinated with the area, and returned on an almost annual basis for many years thereafter.

By 1921, she was so tired of being asked by her New York friends if she had climbed Longs Peak while in Colorado for the summer that she engaged Shep Husted to guide her to the top.

According to some accounts Miss Ferber was a "poor climber," but she did conquer the peak.

Later, in her book *Peculiar Treasure,* she wrote "It wasn't until 1921 that I made it with the aid of Shep Husted. Shep, mountain guide and perfect gentle knight, may be sixty now; he's changeless and seemingly indestructible as Longs Peak itself. Shep is made of iron and gold and granite in pleasing proportions, like the Rockies. He is tireless, dependable, cautious and wise in the ways of the mountains."

All of those attributes served Shep well over the many years he lived and served in the Estes Park area.

In the summer of 1914, Shep Husted outfitted and guided a two week pack trip with three Arapaho Indians through the Estes Park–Grand Lake region. He was chosen because of his reputation as a guide and his familiarity with the local place names.

The trip was arranged in order to learn the Arapaho

names for the area from some Indians who had lived here in their youth, before white settlement.

A 1939 *Estes Park Trail* states, "Shep Husted, veteran guide in the Estes–Rocky Mountain National Park, has climbed Longs Peak 938 times in the fifty-two years that he has spent in the region. He made his last trip up the peak in 1936, but he said that during the summer seasons in years past he has made as many as 26 trips (in a single month) up the 14,255 foot mountain."

Shep was married to Clara Gertrude Crawford on June 29, 1892 in Denver, Colorado, and they homesteaded early in 1893 on Devil's Gulch Road.

Shep had learned the carpenter trade from his Uncle John Cleave (his mother's younger sister, Margaret, was Mrs. Cleave), so they soon had a cabin built for themselves, cottages to rent for summer tourists, and plans begun for building the Rustic Hotel.

The Rustic opened in 1901 and was later sold to Charles Lester who renamed it the Lester Hotel. After his health failed it was bought by the Livingston family, and is now the H Bar G Ranch.

On October 8, 1941, Shep resigned from his duties as general foreman with the Civilian Conservation Corps in Rocky Mountain National Park for health reasons, and the Husteds moved to St. Louis.

They would have celebrated their 50th wedding anniversary in 1942, but Shep died on February 14 of that year at the home of his son, Kenneth, in St. Louis, Missouri.

Many pages could be written about Shep Husted; his friendships, his experiences, his accomplishments. We can't do that now, but we can tell you what these few things written today have to do with this week in our history.

If you don't know already, did you ever wonder how he got the name "Shep"?

What better name could have been chosen for someone destined to lead thousands in a "tireless, dependable, cautious and wise" manner than Shepherd?

Especially if that someone was born on Christmas Day, 1867.

[December 22, 1982]

Abner Sprague's 1930 New Year's Resolution

A new year is upon us!

For some that is a great milestone, a time for celebration, a time for reflection, a time for resolutions in hope of improvement over last year.

For others January 1st is one day after December 31st. Period.

One thing is certain. We're all one or the other, or somewhere in between.

Back when 1930 was fast approaching, A.B. Harris, editor and publisher of the *Estes Park Trail*, asked several local citizens to write a New Year's resolution. One follows.

"This year of 1930 should be a notable one to me, as it is the year in which I pass the four score years of life. In all these years I have never formed the habit of making resolutions at the beginning of the new year. Anyone can realize, if I had done so and lived up to them, I would have passed out years ago, for I would have been too good to live in this wicked world.

"Then it has not been so easy for me to swear off on. I don't make home brew; neither chew nor smoke; I do swear now and then to relieve my blood pressure; for that reason I would not dare to quit that all at once.

"So for the year 1930, I resolve to go on in the same old way and do the best I can—A.E. Sprague."

Abner E. Sprague was born in Dundee, Illinois on March 28, 1850, and came to the Big Thompson Valley in 1864. He first visited Estes Park in 1868, and in 1875 homesteaded in Moraine Park.

He was nearly 17 years old before he went to school. Then, "I decided to study along mathematical lines—surveying, and studies leading to civil engineering. I read everything I could get hold of—good, bad, and worse. I read up on navigation (my father sailed the lakes for nine years), geology, minerology, etc. I don't think that decision was a mistake."

Among the many surveying jobs accomplished by Mr. Sprague were: with the Missouri Pacific Railroad in Nebraska (where he met and married Mary Alberta Morrison), the narrow gauge up Boulder Creek, on the Big Thompson Canyon Road, as Larimer County Surveyor, all over the Estes Park area.

The entertainment of visitors to this area grew, and Sprague's Ranch grew to keep pace. They took on a partner who later bought them out, and it became Stead's Ranch.

After a few years they built a summer cottage in Glacier Basin and "we drifted into entertaining visitors again."

Much of the written history of the Estes Park area was put down by Abner Sprague over the years, and ten years after his 1930 resolution to "go on in the same old way" he produced a short, handwritten autobiography.

In it is some of his philosophy of life.

"If a mistake was made and we do not know what the outcome would have been, why worry. If a decision was a sad mistake, blot it from your memory."

"There is no life but what has been effected for good or bad by the decisions of others."

"You know the world will never be a better world—until each generation are better citizens than their fathers and mothers."

His parents and Abner after them measured with the Golden Rule, and he wrote, "I have always realized that I had a hard example to follow, and also that I have slipped at times: But I ease my conscience by thinking it harder to live up to the Golden Rule now than it was in the old Pioneer days of my parents."

One last item for this week in our history. On December 27, 1943, Abner Sprague died of heart failure at the age of 93 in Denver Presbyterian Hospital.
[December 29, 1982]

BIBLIOGRAPHY

Adams, Henry. *The Education of Henry Adams.* Modern Library, 1931.
Bird, Isabella. *A Lady's Life in the Rocky Mountains.* G.P. Putnam's sons; 3rd ed. Edition, 1881.
Bond, Mrs. C.H. *Highlights of the History of Estes Park.*
Dunning, Harold Marion. *The Life of Rocky Mountain Jim.* Johnson Publishing Company, 1967.
Dunning, Harold. *Over Hill and Vale: In the evening shadows of Colorado's Longs Peak.* Johnson Publishing Company, 1956.
Estes Park Trail-Gazette, May 20, 1921; May 27, 1921; August 19, 1921; August 26, 1921; December 2, 1921; December 16, 1921; March 3, 1922; March 17, 1922; January 19, 1923; January 26, 1923; March 2, 1923; May 25, 1923; November 9, 1923; January 25, 1924; May 23, 1924; June 6, 1924; July 11, 1924; April 17, 1925; July 10, 1925; February 15, 1926; January 21, 1927; February 4, 1927 ; February 11, 1927 ; February 18, 1927; June 10, 1927; July 8, 1927; November 1, 1929; January 22, 1932; February 19, 1932; April 1, 1932; May 20, 1932; January 25, 1935; February 1, 1935; January 3, 1936; July 18, 1941; November 23, 1951; Vacation Edition, 1969
Faber, Edna. *A Peculiar Treasure.* Garden City Books, 1940.
Knapp, Joseph. *The Glen Haven Story.* Johnson Publishing Company. 1967.
Lamb, Elkanah. *Miscellaneous Meditations.* The Publishers' Press Room and Bindery Co., 1913.
Lamb, Elkanah. *Past Memories, Future Thoughts.* United Brethren Pub. House. 1906.
Denver Republican, June 23, 1909; June 24, 1909
Drake Home Demonstration Club (Lindsey, Marguerite ed.). *History of the Big Thompson Canyon.* Larimer County Educational Aids W.P.A. Project, 1940.

Mallett, Richard P. *A Study in Educational Change (1864-1874).*

Mills, Enos Abijah. *The Rocky Mountain Wonderland.* Houghton-Mifflin, 1915.

Mills, Enos Abijah. *The Story of Estes Park and a Guidebook.* 1905.

Mills, Enos Abijah. *The Rocky Mountain National Park.* Houghton-Mifflin, 1932.

Moomaw, Jack C. *Recollections of a Rocky Mountain Ranger.* Times-Call Publishing, 1963.

The Mountaineer, August 13, 1908; August 27, 1908

Peters, Harriet, Dave Stirling, and Rome Richardson. *Rocky Mountainania: A Tenderfoot's Dictionary.* Self-published, 1937.

Richardson, Rome and Clem Yore. *High Country: An Artist's Colorado.* Alden Galleries, 1933.

Rocky Mountain Druggist, July 1909

Rocky Mountain News, September 1, 1868; June 23, 1909

Sprague, Marshall. *A Gallery of Dudes.* Reprint of 1923 edition: University of Nebraska, 1979.

Toll, Oliver W. *Arapaho Names and Trails: Report of a 1914 Pack Trip.* Privately published, 1962.

The Trail, June 29, 1912

The Western Mountaineer, September 6, 1860

Wyndham-Quin, Windham Thomas. *Past and Pastimes.* (Two Volumes) Hodder and Stoughton, 1922.

INDEX

Adams, Charles Francis, 151
Adams, Henry Brooks, 151-155
Adams, John Quincy, 150
Adams, Johnny, 198-201
Adams, President John, 150
Allen, Florence, 45

Boos, Margaret Fuller, 45
Baldpate Inn, 7
Barleen Family Theater, 89
Bear Lake Trail School, 238-239
Beaver Point Association, 177-178
Bierstadt, Albert, 30
Billings, Norton, 15-18
Bird, Isabella, 91, 100-102, 106, 144, 170-173, 186-187, 190-193, 194-197
Blue Jeans Symphony, 89
Bond, Alma, 235-236
Bond, C.H. 77, 83-86, 174, 177, 219, 236
Bond, Florence, 235-236
Bond, Frank, 42, 96-97
Business Men's Association, 234
Byers, William N., 165-168, 180-181

Calhoun, John C., 122, 124
Camp Chipeta, 239
Chamber of Commerce, 93, 182, 202, 214
Chapman, Charles, 13-14
Cheley Colorado Camps, 240
Cheley, Frank, 238-240
Christmas decorations, 229-232
Clatworthy, Fred Payne, 66
Clatworthy, Mrs. Fred P., 4
Collier, Robert Jr., 54
Colorado Country Music Hall of Fame, 89
Colorado Mountain Club, 7, 9, 17, 21, 134-135
Colorado National Forest, see Roosevelt National Forest
Committee of 63, 26
Community and fete day (1925 and 1926), 182-185
Community Church of the Rockies, 210-213
Crispin, Tom, 133-137

Dark Horse Bar, 98
Devil's Gulch, 80-82
Dunraven Cottage, 29
Dunraven Inn, 207

elections, 218-220
electric generator, 241-242
Elkhorn Lodge, 43, 139, 160, 198, 207, 234
English (Estes) Hotel, 29
Eppich, Elinor, 7-8
Estes Park Alikasai, 70
Estes Park Area Historical Museum, 202-204
Estes Park Chalets, 216
Estes Park Fire Department, 40-43
Estes Park Golf and Country Club, 182
Estes Park Library, 234-236
Estes Park Music and Study Club, 87
Estes Park Pioneer Day, 128-132
Estes Park Protective and Improvement Association, 77, 116, 174-179, 234-236
Estes Park Trail-Gazette founded, 70-74
Estes Park Wagon Road Company, 146-148
Estes Park, naming of, 180-181
Estes Valley Improvement Association, 177-178
Estes, Charles Francis, 37-38
Estes, Hardin, 35-36
Estes, Joel Jr., 35-36, 129
Estes, Joel Sr. 35-37, 75, 128-130, 145, 180
Estes, Milton, 35-38, 129
Estes, Patsey (Stollings), 35, 37, 129

Evans, Griff, 101-103, 105-109, 144-145, 155, 170-172

Faber, Edna, 243
Fall River Road, 85-86
Ferguson, Anna, 205-208
fish hatchery, 175-177
Fleming, Mary Louise, 37-38

Garetson, Katherine Griffith, 225-228
Glen Haven, 82
Great Depression, 239
Greene, M. Imogene, 48-51
Griswold, Gun, 133-137, 168

Haberl, Frank J., 32, 214-216
Harris, A.B., 71-73, 246
Hayden, Ferdinand Vandiver, 80
Hix, Charles F., 77
Hondius Ranch, 136-137
Hondius, Eleanor, 159-160, 198-199, 201, 234-235
Hondius, Pieter, 175, 201, 235-236
Hoover, Herbert, 219

Hupp, Josephine, 44, 73
Husted, Shep, 135, 137, 220, 243-245

Ickes, Harold. S., 25

Jackson, Andrew 151
James, H.E., 131
Jefferson, Thomas, 122, 150

Bibliography 253

Jelsema, Ted, 15, 96-98, 239
Johnson, Gov. Ed, 25
Josephine Hotel, 44-45

Kennedy, John F., 220
Kiener, Walter, 7-10
King, Clarence, 153-155

Ladies Aid, 2
Lake Estes, 92-94
Lamb, Elkanah, 19, 156-158
Lawn Lake flood, 178, 242
Lawn Lake, 93-94
Laycook, Barney, 17
Lily Lake Art Studio, 91-92
Lily Lake, 91-93, 136
Lincoln, Abraham, 151
Literary Society of Estes Park, 200
Long, Stephen Harrison, 123-126, 168
Longs Peak House, 19-20, 159
Longs Peak Inn, 7-9, 20, 53, 159, 226
Longs Peak shelter cabin, 52-55
Longs Peak, 7-10, 19, 52-55, 91, 125-126, 135, 154, 158, 161-164, 165-168, 180, 182, 196, 243-244

MacGregor, A.Q., 30, 144-147
MacGregor, Muriel L., 47, 145
McCreery, W.H., 128, 162-164, 218
Mills, Ann, 44

Mills, Enos,
Mills, Enos, 19-21, 26, 44, 60-65, 77, 108-109, 133, 159-160, 225-226, 228
Mills, Joe, 26, 44, 219-220
Monroe, James 122, 150
Moomaw, Jack, 7, 9, 34, 53
Moraine Lodge, 50-51
Muir, John, 20
Music Week in Estes Park, 87-88

National Ski Association, 32
Nixon, Richard, 220
Northern Colorado Road Association, 24-25
Nugent, "Mountain Jim," 80, 91, 100-104, 105-109, 145, 170-173, 186, 196

Olympus Dam, 92-93

Palzer, Victor, 91-92
Peters, Harriet, 67
Pike, Zebulon, 122, 125
Porter, Buel, 229-232
Presbyterian Assembly Association, 82

radio broadcasts, 11-14, 221-224
Riverside Amusement Park, 97-98
Riverside Dance Hall, 99
Rocky Mountain National Park Radio Club, 12
Rocky Mountain National Park Ski Club, 32

Rocky Mountain National Park, 12, 19, 21, 22, 24, 40, 45, 51, 52-55, 60, 76, 177, 239, 244
Rocky Mountain School of Music, 87
Rocky Ridge Music Center, 89
rodeo, 139-143
Rome, Richardson, 66-69
Roosevelt National Forest, 20
Roosevelt, Franklin, 45, 223
Roosevelt, Theodore, 20, 61
Rustic Hotel, 244

Sage, Sherman, 133-137
School Age Ski Tournament (1927), 33-34
Schureman, Rev. W.H., 81-82
Smith, Al, 219
Sortland, Herbert, 8-9, 52, 55
Sprague Hotel, 207
Sprague, Abner, 56-58, 101-102, 109, 145, 147, 246-248
Sprague, Mrs. A. E., 4
Stanley Hotel, 86, 88, 110, 116, 117-121, 139, 214-217
Stanley, F.O., 30, 77, 86, 110-116, 117-118, 120-121, 148, 174-175, 215-217, 241-242
Stanley, Mrs. F.O., 199
Steele, John 15-16
Stirling, Dave, 66-67, 91-92

The Mountaineer, 70
Thompson Canyon Road, 24-26
Timberline Cabin, 8, 53
Toll, Oliver W., 133-137
Toll, Roger, 8-9, 52-53
Townsite Company, 75-76, 85
Trail Talk, 70
Tschudin, Cesar, 17-18

U.S. Forest Service, 20

Vaille, Agnes Wolcott, 7-10, 52, 55

Wagener, Sigfried, 221-224
Weist, Roy, 77
Whyte, Theodore, 29-30
Wilson, Woodrow, 21, 227
Winter Olympics (1932), 15-16
Women's Club, 200, 235
World War II, 221-224
Wyndham-Quin, Windham Thomas (Fourth Earl of Dunraven), 28-31, 75, 80, 105-106, 117, 206

YMCA of the Rockies, 239
Yore, Alberta, 88
Yore, Clem, 67, 88

www.ingramcontent.com/pod-product-compliance
Lightning Source LLC
Chambersburg PA
CBHW031412290426
44110CB00011B/348